10 Ways to a Stronger Marriage

Trey & Lea Morgan

ISBN 9781702369862

www.StrongerMarriageWorkshops.com

The Workshop
StrongerMarriageWorkshops.com

The Book
TheStrongerMarriageBook.com

The Podcast
TheStrongerMarriagePodcast.com

TreyAndLea.com

ACKNOWLEDGEMENTS

So many people have helped us make this book a reality. Thank you to countless friends who have encouraged us over the last few years to put our workshop material in book form and to Steve Hemphill for the inspiration to believe we could really do it. Thank you to many fellow authors who tirelessly answered questions and gave us advice, especially about the publishing process: Michael Whitworth, Tim Archer, Varina Denman, Ron Bruner, Dan Chambers, Steve Hemphill, Alisa Hope Wagner, and Wes McAdams. We offer a big thanks to Rodney & Michelle Gipson, who generously provided a lovely cabin in the beautiful mountains of Ruidoso, New Mexico, so we could concentrate on writing for an entire week. We would like to say thanks to Ray Coates and Susan Green for proofreading and to Peggy Trent Stewart for her expert editing advice. Thank you to Magen Olive for the idea for the book cover and Angie Nichols for helping us tweak the title. Thanks to Connor Morgan for his amazing work on our social media projects. Also, a huge thanks to the good people of Childress. You bless us. We have seen and felt God at work throughout this entire process, and we know His timing for this book is perfect as always. Also, thanks to Cory & Toni Burns, Les Ferguson Jr, Levi Sisemore, Morrisa Summers, Sarah Stirman, Chris Hodges, Warren Baldwin, Jeff Foster, Jeff Smith, and Lee Keele for each taking the time to read a chapter and offer advice.

To our four awesome sons, Taylor, Parker, Connor and Cooper, and our two beautiful daughters-in-laws, Abbey and Callie. Also, to our future grandchildren:

We pray you have strong, healthy marriages for generations and generations to come.

CONTENTS

If you enjoyed this book, please help us support healthy marriages by leaving a positive book review on Amazon. This will help more people find this material when searching for "marriage books" on Amazon.

Thank you,
Trey & Lea

1 – KEEP PADDLING

"Hey Trey, do you want to help me throw out candy at a parade this afternoon?" A friend asked me this question a few years ago, and I wasn't going to refuse an afternoon of fun, candy, and a parade. My friend was a paramedic for the local EMS service, and he had volunteered to take the ambulance over to a neighboring community to throw out candy in their small town's annual parade. I told him I'd love to be his co-pilot.

We arrived about twenty minutes early for the parade and found our position in line with the other first responder vehicles. We were just behind the lone sheriff's vehicle and the volunteer fire department's two old firetrucks. I quickly noted,

"There are not a lot of vehicles or participants in this parade." My friend reminded me that it was a very small community and all he was told was to drive over here, give out all the candy, and hurry back. I looked in the floorboard between the two seats, and there were three of the biggest bags of candy I'd ever seen. I laughed and told my friend, "For a town this size, you may have brought too much candy." We laughed, and he turned on the lights of the ambulance as the parade was starting.

We slowly crept toward Main Street, where the parade was going to take place, made a right turn onto the street and quickly noticed that no one had shown up. Seriously, there were only two or three adults sitting in lawn chairs and one lone kid with a plastic grocery sack that he'd brought to gather up candy. That's it! We laughed and said, "This has got to be the worst parade in the history of all parades!"

I asked what we were going to do with the three massive bags of candy. My friend replied, "I don't know. They just told me not to bring any of it back." We pulled up to the only kid that showed up that day and started dumping handfuls and handfuls of candy on him. We must've sat there for a couple of minutes throwing candy out the window to this kid. Long before we were out of candy, his little sack was full. My friend told me, "Just keep throwing!"

The look on his eleven-year-old face was absolutely priceless. His eyes were as round as silver dollars, and his mouth was wide open. He looked like he'd just won the lottery. He was jumping around, excitedly repeating the same two words over and over, "Oh, wow!" That kid was going to need several plastic sacks to gather up the mounds of candy we'd left all around him. It was quite possibly the greatest day of his entire life.

But then there was a quick turn of events ... what we didn't know was there was actually another turn just around the corner from where this candy-laden kid was. When we rounded the corner, we saw a street lined with people who had shown up for the parade, along with a lot of kids expecting to catch some candy from our ambulance windows. Oh yes, and we were already totally out of candy!

I laugh today thinking that somewhere out in this world is a twenty-something year old guy with a lot of cavities, who still talks about that day being the most amazing day of his childhood.

Marriage books can be overwhelming, at least some have been to me. I've stood there, like that kid at the parade hoping to get a few pieces of candy in my sack to try, and before you know it, I have more information than I'll ever be able to process.

We don't want this to be a book like that. We've tried hard to simply give you ten things you can do to strengthen your marriage. Use this list of ten things as a marriage check-up to help you determine if you are on the right track to building and maintaining a healthy marriage. Our goal is not to overload you, but to give you practical and doable suggestions that you can continue to do on a regular basis.

What we don't want to happen is for this book to become a checklist ... where you check something off and think, "Okay, I've done that. What's next?" Instead, we want this to be a list of suggestions that become regular habits in your marriage, not a one-time-check-it-off-the-list event. These ten healthy things need to be ongoing. Your marriage will be blessed if you continue to do them.

We want to be up front with you from the beginning. We are not licensed professional counselors. We do not have degrees in psychology. We simply have thirty plus years of experience in marriage. We are so grateful that healthy marriages were modeled in the homes we both grew up in. We have a vast number of friends and mentors who have modeled healthy marriages for us. We have learned, through trial and error in our own marriage, what works and what does not work. Believe us, we have made plenty of mistakes along the way. The things we are sharing in this book have worked in our marriage, and we've seen them work in countless other marriages. We strongly believe they will work in your marriage as well.

OUR THROW-AWAY SOCIETY

Does your mother or grandmother wash and reuse disposable cups? Both of our mothers did. They also rinsed and saved aluminum foil and plastic baggies for another use. Our grandmothers lived in a time when cloth diapers were made, used for multiple children, and then used as cleaning rags when all of the kids were finally potty-trained. They got the most use out of everything they owned and took nothing for granted.

Today we live in a throw-away society. So many things are disposable ... dishes, diapers, cameras, contact lenses, razors, water bottles ... the list could go on and on. Even things that are not disposable, like cars and cell phones, some feel the need to upgrade on a regular basis.

Sadly, this disposable mentality has affected even our relationships. When the going gets tough in marriage, some think it's easier to just throw it away and start fresh, rather than value it and make the most of what you already have. We once heard someone give wedding vows that said, "Do you take this woman for better or worse, for richer or poorer, in sickness and health, as long as you both shall *love?*" That is not how God designed marriage. (We will discuss how this is a flawed concept in another chapter.)

In our own vows, we promised to take each other as long as we both shall *live.* We have taken the word divorce completely out of our vocabulary. When things got tough, we muddled through. We promised we would, and we are so glad we did! Our marriage is better now than ever because we didn't give up during the hard times. Throwing our marriage away was never an option. At some point, we can almost guarantee, things will get tough in your marriage. You may be in a tough spot right now. We urge you to never give up.

Satan would love nothing more than for your marriage to fail. He knows that a failed marriage will not only hurt you and your spouse, but it will hurt your kids, other family members, and friends. The damage is far reaching. He wants your marriage because he knows it's extremely valuable. The more marriages he can destroy, the more he weakens society as a whole. *"The thief comes only to steal and kill and destroy"* (John 10:10a, NIV).

Satan will tell you that your marriage is not worth all the trouble you are going through, and that it's just not worth the effort. He will try to convince you it was a mistake, and that it would be easier to just throw it away and start fresh. He is also a liar! *"When he lies, he speaks his native language, for he is a liar and the father of lies"* (John 8:44b, NIV). Marriages are not disposable. They hold great worth and value. They have the ability to bless many generations to come. Your marriage *is* worth fighting for each and every day. Don't listen to Satan's lies. Don't let him win.

REALIZE YOU CAN ONLY CHANGE YOURSELF

We challenge you while reading this book not to point out in your mind the areas where your spouse needs to improve. Instead, ask yourself, "Which of these things do *I* need to work on to improve *myself?*" It is so easy sometimes to read things and think, "I sure wish my spouse would get this through their thick head." As much as you might desperately want your spouse to change, the only person you can change is yourself. You also might be surprised to find that when you begin making changes, you will start to see changes in your spouse as well. In order to get the most out of this book, read it looking for things *you* can do to bless your marriage.

We often say in our workshops that marriage is like two people being in a little rowboat. If both people are paddling, the boat moves amazingly smooth across the water in the direction you want it to go. If only one person is paddling and doing all the work, the little boat does not go anywhere but in circles.

You cannot force your spouse to pick up their oar and row the marriage boat. All you can do is row the marriage boat to the best of your ability, and hopefully that will inspire your spouse to do the same.

You may reach the point of frustration, if you're the only one doing the rowing. It takes two to row a boat and make a marriage work. We urge you in this chapter not to give up. Don't quit! Avoid the temptation to drop your oar and say, "I am done until you pick up your oar and start rowing this boat too!" That's what we call a stalemate in marriage, which is much like a checkmate in chess. Both are killers.

We heard a story years ago about a lady who went to see a counselor because she was frustrated and done when it came to her marriage. She told the counselor, "I need your help. I am in the process of leaving my no-good, dirty, rotten husband. I don't want to just leave him ... I want it to devastate him when I leave. (Nice attitude, huh?)

The counselor said, "I am really into fixing marriages and not helping to destroy them, but I have an idea for you. For the next thirty days, I want you to love your husband amazingly. Be the most incredible wife in the whole world to him. Meet his every need. Serve him hand and foot. Whatever he needs, give it to him."

Of course, she stopped him abruptly and said, "Are you nuts? I don't want to do anything nice for this jerk! I want to do the opposite. I want this to hurt when I leave."

The counselor replied, "Hear me out. Go do all of this, and at the end of thirty days, serve him your divorce papers. He will then realize he has lost the most incredible wife in the world."

She smiled and said, "I love this idea. Thank you," and she headed off to fulfill the plan. The first few days were absolutely torture. Trying to be nice and doing things for a husband who had not put forth any effort in their marriage for the past several years was beyond hard for her. She wanted to give up, but she stuck with it for the entire thirty days.

Several months passed when the counselor ran into the woman at the grocery store. They had not seen one another since her initial visit to his office. The counselor asked, "What happened? Did everything go as planned? Was your husband devastated when you left him?"

She replied, "It did not go anything like you thought. In fact, just the opposite happened. I went home and served him and loved him. It was so hard at first, but after about ten days something changed. He started being nice back to me. I kept up the plan, and after about three weeks, he was doing as many nice things for me as I was for him. Thirty days into this plan, my old husband had returned. In fact, he was better than ever." She added, "It is hard to believe, but our marriage is better today than it has been for the past thirteen years."

The counselor replied, "I'm sure glad things worked out like they did. That is what I was hoping for all along."

Of course, not everything works exactly like this, but it is the perfect example of a stalemate in a marriage. When a wife says, "I am no longer doing anything for him until he starts (fill in the blank)," that is a stalemate. When a husband at the same time says, "I will not do anything for her because she never (fill in the blank)," that is a stalemate. Stalemates are marriage killers.

You can't force your spouse to better your marriage or to make changes. All you can do is pick up your oar, row the boat, and hopefully inspire your spouse to do the same by treating them with love and grace.

It could be that you are in a marriage where you are both rowing and things are going smooth. You may be wondering, "Why should I read this book if we are not currently having any problems?" The reason is that you always want to be working on your marriage. Many married couples don't put any money, time, or effort into their marriage until problems surface. After problems arise, couples frantically start trying to invest time, money, and effort into their relationship in hopes of making it good again. Our point is this: don't wait until your marriage is having issues to start working on it. Work on your marriage during the good times, so there will be less bad times.

We once had a lady contact us and ask if we would be coming to her town to do one of our workshops. "Our marriage needs help," she said. When she stated where she was from, we were a bit confused because we had just been to her town 6 weeks prior.

We replied to her message that we had just been there and apologized that she hadn't known. We always do our best to advertise where we are going to be, but somehow this couple had been missed on our radar. She responded, "Oh I knew you were in town a few weeks back, but we didn't need to go then. Everything was good at that point, but now we've begun to have problems, and we need to know when you're coming back."

We really wanted to say, "If you had attended our workshop when we were in your town six weeks ago, you might not be having these problems now!" We didn't say that, of course, but we cannot stress to you enough how important it is to read a marriage book, attend a workshop, or listen to a good podcast. Do one of these or all of these, but constantly be working on your marriage ... even when things are going well.

Here is another challenge for you: we would love for you to read this book together as a couple. Reading together is one of the best things we have done in our marriage. We don't read out loud to one another, although that would be fine, if that's what you prefer. We take turns reading a chapter or two, and then we discuss what we have read as we go. We underline things that we find important, then we go back and talk about the things we have underlined. It gives us an opportunity to have some good discussions about our marriage.

We are working on our marriage just like you. We are not the perfect couple, nor do we have all the answers. We still have to work hard on our marriage, even after 30 plus years. Please know that while you read this book, we are praying for you. As we stated earlier, the suggestions discussed in this book have worked for us, and they are very practical things that you can do to bless your marriage. You're going to get a LOT of information in this book. Don't be overwhelmed. Just grab your little plastic grocery sack and get ready to catch some good stuff we're going to throw at you. It's going to be a fun ride.

As we mentioned before, marriage is much like a rowboat. It requires two people paddling at the same time for it to work correctly. If only one does all the paddling, the boat goes in a circle, BUT if both are willing to paddle, your little marriage boat will go amazing places. We're praying that both of you are willing to pick up your oar and paddle.

The first thing required in order to build a stronger marriage is a never give up attitude. Don't quit. Keep paddling!

Let us not become weary in doing good, for at the proper time we will reap a harvest if we do not give up.
~Galatians 6:9 (NLT)

2 – KEEP UP THE CHASE

Take a trip down memory lane to the time when the two of you were dating before you were married. Do you remember all the things you did for one another? The very things you did to win your spouse are the very things you need to continue to do to bless your marriage.

Husbands:

- Remember back before you married her how you used to take her on dates? You went on dates at least once a week, and as crazy as it sounds, sometimes several times a week. You looked for every opportunity to spend time with her because you were in pursuit. You went to see movies together, ate dinner together, and did other fun things together. The key word is *together*. You wanted to spend as much time together as you could, and that shouldn't stop once you're married. You should try just as hard to keep her as you did to win her.

- Remember back before you married her, how you used to send flowers and write sweet notes? These were things you did to pursue her. They were a regular part of your relationship before you married, and they shouldn't stop just because she said, "I do."

- Remember back before you married her, how you used to talk all the time? You wanted to get to know her better, so you called, texted, and spent time together asking lots of questions. Communication was how you pursued her. It was a big part of the reason you fell in love with your wife, and it shouldn't stop once you have married her.

- We imagine that before you married her, you held her hand all the time, everywhere you went. You were affectionate. You kissed. You told her she was beautiful. All these things were an important part of your relationship and part of why you fell in love. Affection shouldn't stop once you have married her.

Wives:

- Remember back before you married him, how you flirted with him? You wanted him to know that you were interested. Flirting is how you pursued him. You flirted, and you heaped it on thick. Flirting shouldn't stop once you have married him.

- Remember back before you married him, how you constantly bragged on him about being handsome, strong, sweet, etc.? He absolutely loved hanging out with you because you were always building him up with praise and encouragement. Bragging on him shouldn't stop once you have married him.

- Remember back before you married him, how you dressed up for him? If you were going on a date, or he was coming over, you wanted to look your best. After getting ready for a date, the one thing you wanted to hear from him was, "Wow, you look incredible." Dressing up for him shouldn't stop just because he said, "I do."

Despite what you have heard, love is an action, not a feeling. God created love between a husband and a wife to be an action. Ephesians 5:25 says, *"Husbands love your wives **AS** Christ loved the church, and **GAVE** himself up for her."* (Emphasis ours.) Notice we are to have the same kind of love that Christ has, which is that of giving. Giving is an action.

John 3:16 is a verse that everyone knows, *"For God so loved the world that He gave his one and only Son..."* We see again that love is an action. This kind of love wants the best for the other person involved. When you love the way God intended, you are willing to *do* what's best for the other person involved, whether you feel like it or not.

Feelings can be misleading. We have raised four boys and have jokingly explained to our boys that at some point in their lives, some cute little girl will scoot over really close to them, and that they are going to get all tingly and think, "This feels good. I must love her." We would then remind them that what they would be feeling is not love. What they would be feeling is probably "common sense" leaving their body!

Since love is an action, it has always been a

choice. Remember the wedding vows from chapter one which stated, "as long as we both shall love?" Some people choose to end their marriages because they have "fallen out of love" with one another. They don't understand love as God created it. Love is not something you fall into or out of ... instead, love is a choice. Make the choice every day to love your spouse, even on days when you don't feel it. Notice in the two verses we referenced above that God's love is a choice, not a feeling He has for us. His giving was an action, and that is the kind of love God requires for marriage. Pursuit is an action. You actively pursued your spouse before you married them. You showed them your love by doing things for them. Love was an action for you then, and it should still be.

It was by pursuing your spouse and loving them with actions that you won them in the first place. Sadly, too many couples stop chasing one another once they have been married for a while. They stop pursuing. Continuing to pursue one another will keep your marriage fresh, vibrant, and fun. Too many couples get comfortable after they have been married for a while and stop doing the very things that caused them to "fall in love" with one another. "Comfortable" is for old house shoes and recliners, not for marriage.

Please don't misunderstand what we are saying here. You should be comfortable with each other because you have built a friendship and a level of intimacy, but becoming too comfortable to the point of laziness in your marriage can be a marriage killer. Don't get lazy and stop trying. If you work as hard to keep your spouse as you did to win them in the beginning, your marriage will be absolutely amazing.

Maybe you have found yourself getting too comfortable in your marriage. Maybe you have moved your marriage to the back burner for less important things in this world, or maybe you have had to move your marriage to the back burner for necessary and unavoidable things. If so, it's probably time for an adjustment in priorities and time to make some changes.

The next several sections will give you some detailed practical ways to keep up the chase.

Date

Dating is important because it is fuel for your marriage. It is when you get to spend time alone with your spouse. "Due to jobs, kids, TV, the internet, hobbies, and home and family responsibilities, the average married couple spends just four minutes a day alone together."[1] This is an astounding statistic! A couple needs time alone together with no distractions, when no one is looking at a cell phone, laptop, video game, TV screen, etc. Four minutes a day is not sufficient to build a healthy marriage, but when you are dating regularly, you are increasing the opportunity for your marriage to grow.

We get a lot of pushback from couples when we say dates should happen once a week because they say they don't have the time or money for it, but let us explain what we mean by "dating." We are not talking about going out on an expensive, dress-up date every week. Dates don't have to be elaborate or expensive. Some weeks it can be as simple as meeting for lunch while the kids are at school. You can order off the dollar menu or have a picnic at the park. You can simply put the kids to bed and spend time playing a board game or cards together. You can go on an evening walk together. Some of our very best conversations happen during evening walks!

Not everything has to be a fancy date, but a fancy date is important on occasion. It is healthy to dress up and go to the concert, or the weekend away that you have planned and saved for. We met a couple recently who said, "We had so much fun back when we were dating." Our response was,

"Why have you stopped?"

Another big kicker or pushback when it comes to dating weekly is childcare. The old "where do we find a babysitter" ordeal is legitimate. Of course, it is always handy if you have family or grandparents close by to watch the kids, but not everyone does. Yes, babysitting can be expensive!

Have you considered a babysitting swap with friends who have children about the same age as your kids? Ask them to watch your kids on Friday night so you can go on a date, and then reciprocate by watching their kids on Saturday night so they can go on a date. You just scored free babysitting, and your kids will have a blast playing with their friends while you are away. Boom! We used to swap babysitting with friends regularly, and it worked great for us.

INSTANT MARRIAGE BOOST:
Look at your calendar right now and plan a date for this week!

One more rule on dating is that double dates don't count. Going out with friends doesn't count as a date because you know what happens when you double date? The guys hang out together and visit, and the girls hang out together and visit, and you don't get any one-on-one time as a couple. It's healthy to enjoy an occasional double date with friends, but don't count it as a date night.

Sadly, the average couple dates only once a month, if even that often. Once a month is better than never dating, but work hard to shoot for once a week.

12 GREAT DATE NIGHT IDEAS

GET FANCY: Get dressed up and go to a nice restaurant and a play or a concert.

MOVIE NIGHT IN: Watch a romantic movie and cuddle on the couch.

FIRST DATE: Try to recreate your first date as much as possible.

SWEAT FEST: Catch a brisk walk or run, or go to the gym for a good workout; then shower together when you get home.

BLACKOUT: Spend the evening at home forbidding the use of electricity or phones! Eat sandwiches and play your favorite game by candlelight.

SWEET MEMORIES: Enjoy an evening looking at old photos and memorabilia. Watch your wedding video, if you have one.

SUNDAY DRIVE: Pick up a coffee or soda, then go for a drive though a pretty local neighborhood or out in the country to take in some scenery.

BRIGHTEN SOMEONE'S DAY: Make cookies together, then deliver a few to a widow or widower, and spend some time chatting with them.

PICNIC: Pack a lunch and go to your local park. After eating, feed the ducks, swing at the playground, and go for a walk.

GET THRIFTY: Go to a flea market or thrift store. Set a price limit and purchase the most meaningful and creative gift for each other that you can find.

BIKE IT: Go for a bike ride and stop off for some ice cream.

DINNER & DESSERT: Cook dinner together and be sure to have one another for dessert later.

Flirt

Don't ever stop flirting with your spouse. Flirting is a healthy part of your marriage. Wives, you flirted with your husband pre-marriage, and you should still be flirting with your husband. We have yet to ever hear a husband say, "I hate it when my wife flirts with me." He likes it; he really does. There are so many ways that you can flirt with your husband.

- Meet him at the door with a really good kiss

when he comes home.

- When you're out on that date, or even better, out in a group, take your foot and rub his leg under the table. (Let us add a Marriage "Pro Tip" here: if you are with a group, make sure you are rubbing *his* leg and not someone else's! ☺)

- Use your phone to send your spouse a sweet or sexy text message. Husbands, send her a "have an awesome day" text. Wives, send him a text that says, "I have sure been missing you today and can't wait to see you this evening." Wives, you will get bonus points if you send him a spicy text message. He will most likely love it.

A couple who attended one of our workshops shared with us how they were good at flirting with one another using their phones. She made the comment, "About once a week I like to lay out something very lacy and/or sheer on the bed. I simply take a picture of the item and send it to my husband with the message 'I plan on wearing this to bed tonight.'" She smiled and said, "Every time I do this, two things are guaranteed to happen. First, he is going to come home early from work. Second, he is going to come home in a great mood." It was at that point her husband piped up and said with a happy smile on his face, "I have a hard time concentrating at work on the days she does this."

Do Unexpected Little Things

Too many husbands buy flowers only for special occasions such as anniversaries, Valentine's Day, or when they are in the doghouse. Guys, surprising your wife regularly and for no reason at all will let her know that you love her. If she likes flowers, by all means, buy the flowers, but make sure you know your wife and know what she likes.

Lea is not a flower kind of girl, or rather, she is not a fan of big expensive bouquets of flowers. I had to learn this as her husband, and honestly, it took me a while. While I was thinking that I had done well by purchasing a big bouquet of flowers, she was thinking to herself, "I could've bought a lot of groceries for what he spent on flowers that are going to die in a week." I have learned over time that Lea absolutely loves getting a single rose. It is definitely much cheaper, and she is a frugal girl, but if your girl is a "big bouquet of flowers" kind of girl, then buy the flowers, and do it for no real reason at all other than to show love.

Lea is more of an ice cream or chocolate kind of girl. I can pretty much make her day by simply stopping at an ice cream shop or adding her favorite candy bar to the bag of groceries she has sent me to the store to pick up. The point is, husbands, make sure you are romancing your wife her way.

Men often think of romance in a sexual way. If the subject of romance came up, I used to think it had something to do with sex, but romance to a woman can mean something entirely different. I once asked Lea while we were driving down the road, "What are some things that I do that you find romantic?" She started naming off stuff that had nothing to do with sex, or so I thought. "When you fill my car up with gas, so I don't have to," and "When you run the vacuum at the house when the floors are dirty," were two things that she listed very quickly.

I remember saying to her, "Seriously, those things don't have anything to do with sex." I believe her reply was, "They do; just not in the way you see it." I learned something about romance that day, and what my wife thinks is romantic. She likes to be served. She likes for me to show her through action that I love her and want to take care of her.

Husbands, another little thing your wife is sure to

love is holding her hand. It has been said that most women need ten non-sexual touches a day. Meaning, she needs to be touched, hugged, etc. without any intention that it will lead to sex. Someone said recently that women need a seven-second hug when they come home from work and haven't seen you all day long. Husbands, I know you're thinking that seven seconds is forever, but it's really not.

Be sure to brag on her cooking, or brag on anything that she does for that matter. Make sure she hears you say things like, "I definitely married up." Remind her that she's beautiful. Tell her you are amazed by her curves, and make sure she knows you are still attracted to her. Use your words to build up your wife.

Men, if your job requires you to wear scrubs, overalls, or something else of that sort, dress up for her occasionally. Many women think their man looks especially sexy in a pair of slacks and a nice shirt or even a jacket and tie.

Wives, you can do all of these same things. The things you did pre-marriage should continue after you're married. Dress up for him on occasion. It seems like when we get home from a long day the first thing we want to do is get out of our nice clothes and into something comfortable.

Comfortable generally means pajama bottoms, house shoes, or an oversized sweatshirt. Before marriage, we saw each other dressed up more than dressed down. After marriage, that often reverses. Men especially seem to be very visual, so make sure you aren't always dressing down when you are together.

Brag on him a lot. (We will talk in detail about this in chapter three.) Cook for him. Make his favorite dessert. After all, the way to a man's heart, as they say, is through his stomach.

Marriage should be about celebrating your love for one another often, for no reason other than you love each other. Don't wait for your anniversary or Valentine's Day to go on a date. Go ahead and buy the roses, light the candles, use the nice sheets, wear the fancy lingerie! Don't save those things for just special occasions. Celebrate your love and marriage regularly. (We encourage you to re-read this paragraph and underline it.)

Personally, I love when Lea brags on me about being a good dad around our boys. I love when she tells me that I still look good to her after 30 years of marriage. I love how she brags on me for even the small things that I do. It simply motivates me to want to do them better and more often.

On our twentieth anniversary, Trey approached

me and mentioned that he wanted to start doing something new for me. I wasn't exactly sure what he meant, but I was interested. He simply said, "I have been trying to figure out a new way that I can show you how much I love you." I did not realize that he had been thinking about this for a long time. He finally explained to me that from this day forward, he wanted to start opening the car door for me wherever we went. I wasn't going to complain about that; I thought it was sweet. He did tell me that he was going to need my help. "In twenty years of marriage, I have never done this, so it is not going to be something that I just start and never forget. I am going to need you to help remind me when I forget, so I can make it a habit."

Over the next few weeks he did fantastic, but there were times he would forget because it's not easy developing a new habit. I would simply remind him, and he would thank me for it. (I once reminded him by allowing him to get all the way into the car and put the key in the ignition. Then he looked over and realized I was still standing outside the car, by the door, waiting on him to come open it. That one really helped him remember.)

It's been over ten years since Trey started doing that. I love how it makes me feel special and cared for, but our favorite thing about the whole door-opening scheme has been our sons' reaction to it. Over the last ten years, our boys have watched their father open the door for their mother everywhere they go. They have learned that opening the door for Mom is just something that someone is supposed to do. We noticed a few years ago that anytime we went out as a family somewhere, Trey rarely got the opportunity to open my door because one of the boys would beat him to it. Trey loves the fact that he has taught his boys how to treat their future wives. He loves the fact that one day he is going to have a daughter-in-law who is going to say, "Your son is so good to me. Did you know he opens the car door for me?"

Husbands, your children are learning about marriage from watching how you treat their mother; and wives, your children are learning how to treat their future spouse by watching how you treat their father. It is imperative that we teach our children well. Do the little things in your marriage ... because they are actually the big things.

Have you ever thought about your funeral - what it will be like or what you want to be said? Being a minister, I have given a lot of eulogies at funerals. I have noticed that out of all the funerals that I have done and have attended, no one ever talks about what kind of car the deceased person drove. They don't spend much time talking about their degrees or how much money they had in their bank account. The focus tends to be on their relationships. Relationships are by far the most valuable things that you have on this earth. It is not your business or your material things. Instead, it is your relationships. Sadly, too many people fail to see this until they have lost a relationship.

Personally, I think the greatest things that can be said at any funeral are related to relationships. I will be perfectly content as a successful man if someday at my funeral someone stands up and only says, "Trey loved God. He absolutely adored his wife, and he loved his children." I'd love at this point for the speaker to simply say, "The funeral is over. Now let's go have some barbecue." There's really nothing greater that could be said. It is all about loving those that God gave you ... and loving them well.

A few years ago, I did a funeral for a man who had been married to his wife for fifty-five years. After the end of the service, I found myself standing at his casket along with his wife. She was trying to figure out how to say her last goodbye before they closed her husband's casket for the final time. She looked at me, smiled and said, "Trey, I know I told you we'd been married for fifty-five years, but it wasn't just any fifty-five years. It was fifty-five really good years. He kissed me every night at bedtime and hugged me every morning when we got up. He faithfully sent me flowers every month, and he still told me every day that I was beautiful."

I felt as if I was listening in on a private conversation as she continued to tell me, "He often called me Hazel." I asked how she got that nickname and she said, "My eyes are hazel, and he always told me how beautiful my eyes were." I smiled as my heart ached for her. It was then she continued to talk, but now she spoke to him and not to me. "Thank you for being so good to me," she said with tears and a smile. "I will miss you, and I will see you soon." She patted him on the hand, kissed him on the forehead one last time, then nodded to me and said softly, "Okay, I'm ready. Let's go."

As I drove to the cemetery to say some final words to the family, I realized that I had been privileged to witness a very holy last moment between a husband and his wife. I couldn't help but be thankful and inspired by this man whom I barely knew, and who was no longer alive. I sat for a moment by myself to collect my thoughts ... and then I prayed, "Lord, please raise up more men who will hug their wife every morning, kiss her every night and remind her every day that she's beautiful ... and Lord, please make me one of those men."

Choose your Love; Love your choice.

~Thomas S. Monson

3 – TALKING IS NOT OPTIONAL

Lea and I married in the late 1980s just out of high school. We had dated for four years before we got married. We love reminiscing about dating back in the '80s. I imagine your dates were similar to ours. There were times we would watch a movie. We usually went to the one-dollar movie theater, so we would have enough money to go to a restaurant, but what we really wanted to do was talk and spend time together. We were just getting to know one another, so we would spend lots of time talking.

I remember going to her house to pick her up for a

date we had planned. I would say hello to her parents and find out what time she needed to be home. She would usually appear from the bathroom ten minutes or so after she told me she would be ready. (I should have recognized that as a prediction of future events because she is not an "on-time" person. ☺) When she was finally ready, we would say goodbye to her parents and head out for an evening of fun.

Many of our dates included fast food, a blanket, and a park where we could have a picnic. We would literally sit for the entire evening just talking. We were trying to get to know one another. I remember asking questions like, "What's your favorite ice cream flavor?" and "What are your favorite TV shows?" I found out she liked the combination of chocolate and orange sherbet together, and she loved watching the TV series *Moonlighting*, starring Bruce Willis and Cybill Shepherd. We would simply talk and exchange information. We talked about the future, our dreams, and even how many kids we wanted to have some day.

I was always amazed at how quickly time would fly on those dates. We might have been there for two or three hours just talking, but it would seem like twenty to thirty minutes. On many occasions, we would check the time and realize we needed to hurry to get her home in time for her curfew. I would drive her back to her house, get the kiss on the front porch that I wanted really badly, and I would tell her goodnight.

After arriving at my own house, which was usually dark because everyone was already asleep, I would head to the kitchen to raid the refrigerator. I still vividly remember many times walking past the phone hanging on the kitchen wall. (Yes, phones used to hang on walls! For those of you under the age of thirty, you may need to Google "telephone on wall" so you can understand. This is real stuff that existed in the '80's. I'm not making this up!)

I would walk past the phone and think to myself, "It seems like forever since I've talked to Lea. I would sure love to call her." (For those of you under 30, the only thing you could do with this phone that was attached to the wall was make phone calls. You could not check Facebook; you could not update Twitter, and you could not text with it. It made phone calls ... only phone calls.)

I wanted to call her that night, but it was late. I knew there would be a phone in her room that she might answer, but I also knew there was a phone in her parents' room as well. Calling would be a big gamble, but it would be worth it, if the love of my life would pick up.

Before I started dialing, I gave myself the following two rules. First, if it rings more than once, I will hang up. Second, if anyone other than Lea answers, I will also hang up. (These phones that hung on walls in the '80s also did not have caller ID.)

I placed my finger in the little circular dial of the phone and dialed all seven numbers. After the seventh number, with sweat beads on my forehead, I heard a ring, and the cute little brown-eyed, brown-haired girl that I hoped would answer, did so. This phone, which was attached to the wall, had an extremely long phone cord allowing me to lay down on the floor while talking. I remember after one three-hour date of nothing but conversation, we talked on the phone for another hour that night.

Today we often laugh about this story and wonder, "What in the world did we talk about for that long?" But, when it comes right down to it, we fell in love because we *talked* to one another. We were attracted to one another, but we didn't fall in love because of attraction. We fell in love through *conversation,* and when we continue to regularly talk and communicate, we keep that love alive. Catch this ... this is really important: Communication to a marriage is like oxygen to life. Without it, it dies.

Don't Expect Him to Just Know Things, Tell Him

Women are naturally instinctive. They often pick up on what someone needs or wants without much conversation. Men are to the other extreme, and women often struggle with this. Men do not do well with hints or having to connect the dots. Men are not wired that way. God did not create men to be instinctive like women. So wives, get this, the best thing you can do for your husband is tell him *exactly* what it is you need or want from him.

Don't make him try to read your mind, string together hints, or connect the dots. You can't get the dots close enough for him to understand what you're trying to get across. Just tell him. By the way, as frustrating as it might be, you'll probably have to tell him more than once.

We once met a lady at one of our workshops who said, "I have been married to my husband for thirty years, and he should be able to know what I need by now." We assured her that she could be married for *one hundred* and thirty years, and he still won't have a clue what she needs unless she specifically tells him. (If by chance you married a man who is instinctive and knows what you need without saying anything, hang on to him because you got a one-in-a-million rare catch.) If you want your spouse to know how you feel or what you need, telling them works better than waiting for their telepathic powers to kick in.

Share Your Heart: Whether You Understand Her Need for It or Not

Someone once said that men speak about 12,000 words a day, while women speak about 25,000. I like to say that women speak twice the amount of words as men because we women have to repeat everything we say! Trey jokingly loves to say that women speak 25,000 words a day with gusts up to 30,000. If this is true, a husband has used up his 12,000 words by the time he gets home from work.

Maybe that's why when your husband comes home from work and you ask him how his day was, he simply responds with, "Good." If you ask him a follow-up question like, "What did you do today?" he again will respond with another single word answer, "Nothing." You see, men are simply out of words by the time they get home from work. Okay, we really do know this is not true, but it does make me wonder sometimes, as a wife, if it is.

Silliness aside, Trey and I struggled greatly with open communication as a young and newly married couple. I would often ask Trey when he came home from work, "What did you do today? He would respond with, "Nothing." Every day I got this same one-word answer. I knew he had to be doing something because he was gone all day! My young immature mind started wondering, "Is he hiding something he doesn't want me to know?" Of course, he wasn't, but he honestly thought the details of his day would bore me.

He didn't understand that I actually did care, and that I didn't think his day was boring at all. He didn't consider that I had been home with two toddlers all day, doing things like changing diapers, watching Barney on TV, and having child-like conversations. I was longing for some adult conversation. I was longing for communication from my husband. I wanted to know what he had done all day, not because I was prying, but because I wanted to feel like I had been a part of his day by knowing the details.

Thankfully, over time, Trey caught on. Fast forward thirty years ... now when he comes home and I ask, "What did you do today?", he never fails to give me all the details of his day. He has come to realize this is important to me.

Husbands, get this: Trey still probably doesn't understand why I enjoy knowing about his day, but he is more than happy to share the details with me because he knows it's what I like. You don't always have to understand what your spouse needs in order to happily give it to them and meet that need. You do it because you want what is best for your spouse. So, husbands, share your heart with her, whether you understand why it is important or not. Don't think that communication is overrated or unnecessary. Your marriage needs communication as much as you need air to breathe. When she asks, "What did you do today at work?", don't respond, "Nothing." Instead, give her all the details. Put away the electronics, TV, etc. and make an effort to communicate with her.

Men compartmentalize every aspect of their life. There is a work compartment, a home compartment, a hobby compartment, a friend compartment, and the list goes on. Women don't think like this. Every part of their life intermingles with the others. Home, work, kids, friends, projects ... it's all one big beautiful bowl of potpourri. This is why we can multitask while talking about ten different subjects all at once! Men just can't do that. They need to focus on one thing at a time. Don't overwhelm them with too much information all at once, or they might just tune you out.

Also, keep in mind that communication doesn't always come easy to some men. Men are comfortable passing along facts but often struggle with deep conversation. Men, this is not a pass for you to avoid communicating with your wife. Realize your wife probably needs more than just facts and information from you, she needs meaningful conversations.

Coffee Time

Over the years, one of the things we have done right is set aside about thirty minutes a day for conversation. We call it our "coffee time." It started years ago when our boys were small. Trey's schedule was flexible enough that he could leave his office and pick up the boys from school since I often had a little one still at home napping. He would drop the boys off at the house before returning back to work. Sometimes he would have me start some coffee, so he could grab a cup before heading back to the office.

Eventually we began having a cup of coffee together every day when he dropped the boys off. This became an important time of the day that we looked forward to because it was our time to check in with one another. We would have about thirty minutes to just visit, talk about upcoming schedules. We still have coffee time to this day at about 3:30 every afternoon. If we come home to a house full of boys, we make coffee and head to our bedroom or the patio where it is quiet because it is our time. Even though our nest is almost empty, our boys all know that we still have coffee time together at 3:30 each and every day.

You need to find some coffee time in your marriage. Coffee is optional, but you need a little portion of the day alone with your spouse just to talk, reconnect, and discuss schedules. Maybe in the morning before you leave for work is a better time for you, or after you get kids to bed, but find some time every day to have "coffee time" together. It will bless your marriage.

INSTANT MARRIAGE BOOST:

If you don't already have a set time every day to "check in" with each other, think about your daily schedule right now and decide a good time to do this.

CONVERSATION STARTERS

FOR COUPLES

1 - What is your favorite color?

2 - What is your favorite candy bar?

3 - What is your best childhood memory?

4 - What is your worst childhood memory?

5 - Did you ever get in trouble in school?

6 - If we could take a trip anywhere and money was not an issue, where would you choose?

7 - What is your favorite season?

8 - In your opinion, what is the most romantic thing we've ever done?

9 - If you had to write one sentence to be put on your tombstone, what would you want it to say?

10 - What is the best advice you were ever given? Who gave it to you?

A Sure Way to Hurt Your Marriage in One Easy Step

There are some poor forms of communication out there. One of them is the silent treatment. It is a horrible form of communication that does only harm. If you want to destroy your marriage in one easy step, regularly use the silent treatment on your spouse.

There will be times when you will be upset, and you might need to tell your spouse, "Give me some time to cool off before we talk." This is different from the silent treatment because you take time to explain to your spouse that you need time to be silent in order to keep you from saying things you might regret. However, the silent treatment, or simply ignoring your spouse in an angry fashion, is an extremely poor way to inform your spouse that something is wrong. It hurts your marriage more than it makes a point. If your spouse asks you if something is wrong, do not say, "NO!" when there actually is something wrong. Don't make them spend the day guessing what is wrong. If something is wrong, simply tell them.

Using the wrong tone is another poor form of communication. We heard years ago that 10% of conflict is due to difference in opinion, while 90%

is due to the wrong tone of voice. When trying to talk to your spouse about something, think about how you like to be talked to. Your tone matters! The Bible states, *"A soft answer turns away wrath, but a harsh word stirs up anger."* (Proverbs 15:1, ESV) Never let a bad day at work, rush hour traffic, moodiness, PMS, a bad day on the golf course, or anything else affect the way you treat your spouse and family. Don't be unkind or speak harshly to those who are most likely innocent. Watch your tone.

4 Ways to Improve Your Communication:

- **PAY ATTENTION:** When your spouse is talking, make sure you are paying attention. Make sure you and your spouse are listening to one another. You cannot do this if you're looking at your phone, TV, computer or video game. Stop what you're doing, make eye contact, and give your spouse your total attention and the respect they deserve.

  I have really struggled with this at times with Lea. I often think I have the ability to multitask while listening to her, but I really don't. Recently, I was trying to listen to something she was saying and text at the same time. I heard her say to me, "You haven't heard a single word I've said, have you?" I looked up from my phone and thought, "That's an odd way for her to start a conversation." Nope, I hadn't heard a word. I apologized, and I am working to do better on this.

- **CONTROL YOUR EMOTIONS:** Personally, we don't feel like there is EVER a time for yelling, calling names, or throwing things. It simply does not set the tone for better marriage communication. Keep your tone calm and loving. Stay in control of your emotions.

- **PUT YOURSELF IN THE OTHER PERSON'S SHOES:** Try to see each issue from your spouse's point of view. Hear them out, and don't think of what you're going to say next while they are still talking. Steven Covey said, "Seek first to understand, then to be understood."[1]

- **PLAN:** Set a daily time for conversation. Whether it's around the dinner table, over a cup of coffee or a few minutes each night before bed, always make time to check in with one another. Questions like, "How was your day?" or "How are you feeling?" or "What do you think about this?" should be regular questions.

Talking to your spouse is essential. When your spouse asks about your day, take the time to tell them. When you ask about their day, pay attention to what they say. Take time to get to know your spouse all over again. Your spouse's likes and dislikes might change over time, so continue to be a student of them. Ask them simple things like, "What's your favorite ice cream flavor?" You might just find out that chocolate and orange sherbet has been replaced with butter pecan.

Ultimately the bond of all companionship, whether in marriage or in friendship, is conversation.

~Oscar Wilde

4 – HEAP IT ON THICK

One of the greatest things you can do to bless your marriage is give one another lots of praise. Have you ever noticed how newlyweds seem to overlook the things that get on each other's nerves and constantly praise the things they love about each other instead? They will go on and on about how awesome their spouse is, often times almost causing you to roll your eyes because they talk about their spouse like they are almost perfect. You can't help but think to yourself, "Just give it a little time, and you'll be out of the newlywed stage soon." Newlyweds praise one another, and they heap it on really thick. They praise one another in private and in public.

As the marriage goes along, we often tend to do the exact opposite that newlyweds do. Instead of overlooking the things that get on our nerves and focusing on what our spouse does right, we tend to focus on the things that really get under our skin and take for granted the things they do well. We even go so far as to think we are doing our spouse a favor by pointing out their flaws hoping they will improve. These are unhealthy habits to fall into in marriage. People who have been married for any length of time could learn something from newlyweds like:

* Focusing on the good things our spouse does.

* Overlooking the things that get on our nerves.

* Giving praise ... lots and lots of praise.

There are a lot of things you can say to build up your spouse. HUSBANDS, here are a few things that your WIFE would probably LOVE to hear from you:

- You are simply amazing.
- I love you. I'm so blessed to be married to you.
- You look amazing.
- You are my best friend.
- Thank you for all you do for our family.
- Let's go on a date.
- I'm so glad you are mine.

- Let's talk.
- I'll cook tonight.
- I love your curves.

WIVES, here are a few things that your HUSBAND would probably LOVE to hear from you:

- You are my hero.
- Let's make love.
- Let's do something together.
- I love you.
- I love being your wife. I'm the luckiest girl in the world.
- You are a great lover.
- I respect you.
- You look amazing.
- I'd marry you all over again.
- You still turn me on.

The Bible clearly and plainly tells us, *"Do not use harmful words, but only helpful words, the kind that build up and provide what is needed, so that what you say will do good to those who hear you."* *(Ephesians 4:29, GNT)* Despite the fact that we are told not to use "harmful words," we tend to be really good at critiquing.

INSTANT MARRIAGE BOOST:

Write your spouse a sweet note or send them a text message right now!

Praise vs. Criticism

The choice is yours. Will you use the majority of your words to build up your spouse and children, or will you use them to criticize? Quite honestly, no one wants to be married to a critic. A study has shown that couples are much less likely to divorce when they give five times more praise than they do criticism.[1] We like those odds. We need to be doing a lot more praising and much less criticizing.

Praise comes easy to some but is a struggle for others. Trey is a glass half full person. He is naturally optimistic and always sees the good in things. He is the cheerleader in our family, regularly reminding everyone just how awesome we are. I, on the other hand, am more of a glass half empty person, who naturally tends to be more pessimistic and negative. Praise does not come easy for this type of personality. I have learned that I do not have to say everything I think, meaning I can keep my negativity and criticism to myself most of the time. It has been something that I've had to work at really hard. If you are a glass half empty person, you understand this. We have to be very intentional in giving more praise and less criticism.

We discussed in the introduction that you cannot force your spouse to paddle their side of the marriage boat. Nor can you use criticism to force your spouse to change something you do not like without causing issues in your marriage, but you _can_ use praise to change your spouse. We sometimes mistakenly think we are actually helping our spouse by pointing out their flaws, but that usually ends up hurting them instead. Catch them doing what you like and praise them for it. When that takes place, change happens without resentment and hurt.

There is a chair in our bedroom that was put there to sit on, but the only things that really sit on that chair are Trey's clothes. He has a system with his clothes…levels of dirtiness, as he calls it. The clothes in the chair are not clean enough to hang up in the closet but are not dirty enough to go into the dirty clothes hamper. You may have a chair just like this in your bedroom. For us, this chair has been a source of irritation in our marriage at times.

Early in marriage, I would use criticism to try to get

him to work on the pile of clothes that were in the chair when they reached a certain height. It usually just caused more arguments. There was also a time when I just chose to ignore the chair altogether. I thought it was better to ignore it than to fight about it. I often wondered if I didn't say anything at all, would he just let the clothes get all the way to the ceiling?

Then, one day, I walked in and he was cleaning up the chair! Instead of saying something like, "It's about time you clean that mess up!" I said something along the lines of, "You are so awesome to clean up the chair. You don't know how much it helps me to know what is clean and what is dirty. Thank you for being so good to me."

What I noticed when I gave him praise instead of criticism is that he picked them up again the next day. I continued to give more praise than criticism until the chair these days is virtually clear. (Virtually means much clearer than it used to be, and a person could actually sit there if necessary.☺)

Work on using praise to build up your spouse and to help change behaviors. Like a newlywed, notice what your spouse is doing well and praise them for it. If you are willing to do that, they will be more willing to continue doing positive things.

Husbands Are Motivated by Praise

As crazy as it may sound, your husband's self-confidence and self-worth rises and falls on whether or not you are giving him regular praise or criticism. Re-read that last sentence again. It is that important. You have the power and ability to help create a husband who believes he is a super dad and a super husband. You can tell your husband something like, "You are the best dad in the world. Our children are blessed to have such an awesome father." Then you may just find him spending the next three hours wrestling on the floor with the kids because he is beginning to believe that he is a great dad. You have the ability to bring that out in him.

Wives, have you noticed how your husband can do the simplest chore around the house, and he will come to tell you what he's done ... wanting some praise or a pat on the back? You may be thinking, "Yes, and if I sought him out to tell him every time I did something around the house, I would never get anything done." The reason your husband points out something he's done is because he loves it when you give him praise. He is simply wanting you to say, "Well done." He tells you because he loves your praise and appreciation of him that much.

Remind him that he is still handsome, that he is a good man, that he still turns you on, etc. He regularly needs to hear these things. When he does little things to serve you or surprise you, make a big deal out of it. Tell him he is awesome, heap on the praise, and you will find him doing it again and again. Even for a normal thing he does on a regular basis, praise him. When he finishes mowing the lawn, tell him that it's the best you have ever seen the yard look. When he fills up your car with gas, opens the door for you, or carries in groceries for you, remind him again just how good he is to you. You are helping to build up a man who will want to be a super husband. He is motivated by your praise.

We have some friends in our community that we have been friends with for 30 years. Paul called one day and asked if I had any time to help him build a backyard fence. I told him my schedule was clear, and I could be there first thing the next morning.

When I got there, Paul had all the supplies and tools laid out, so we could go right to work. We had been working for about 30 minutes when Paul's wife, Stacey, came out to look at our progress. Stacey was excited about the new fence. On her first time out, she noticed that one of the posts was not straight and made a comment about it. I explained that the hole didn't have concrete yet, and we assured her that it would be straight before we started putting the fence up. Stacey came out again about 30 minutes later and pointed out something else that was a little off. It was totally okay that she was doing this. It was her fence, and she wanted it to be perfect. The third time she came outside, I thought, "I am going to have a little fun."

I stopped her before she could say anything and said, "Did you know that this is your third time to come out here, and you have yet to tell me I am doing a good job? I am totally okay with you pointing out things we need to fix, but I also need you to give me some praise, so I can stay motivated to stay here and help." She quickly replied, "You ARE doing awesome. I thought you knew that. I want you to stay as long as possible and help get this fence up." I reminded her that it was good to hear that from her and that her praise motivated both of us to keep working.

I quickly became amused because literally ten minutes later she came out, looked at an area of the fence, and said "You guys are doing an absolutely fantastic job. I am impressed," then went back inside the house. I noticed immediately that her husband, Paul, walked over to the same area she had just commented on, looked it up and down and said, "That IS a good-looking fence." I smiled and said nothing. I could tell he enjoyed hearing his wife's praise.

Pretty much every 15 minutes on the dot, Stacey would come out, look at how we were doing and comment about how awesome everything looked. I would smile when she came out knowing what she was going to say. It was becoming a game between us, but at the same time, I noticed Paul had become extremely motivated by her praise. Every time she came out, he also would look at the fence and talk about how good it looked. He was quickly turning into the Superman of fence builders because of her praise. He even asked if I could possibly stay and work through lunch. He was enjoying building a fence for his wife.

When Stacey finally left for work, I thought to myself, "Okay, no more games. We can finally get some work done." She had done a fantastic job giving us praise for the last hour. She wasn't gone but fifteen minutes when I noticed Paul reach into his pocket, pull out his cell phone, and read a text with a grin on his face. I inquired as to who it was, and he said, "It was Stacey. She said that she can see the progress of the fence all the way from her office, and we are doing a fantastic job," and then he continued, "This is a great fence. Let's keep working!" All it took was a little praise from his wife to keep him going.

Wives, your husband is motivated by your praise. Heap it on thick!

You Married a Daughter of The King, Treat Her as Such

Of course, women need praise too! If she is constantly being told ways she can improve, her self-confidence will waver. She needs praise for being a great mom and a great wife. Remind her regularly that she is an awesome cook, and that you are still amazed by her curves. Your wife should never be the butt of your jokes. She should never be made fun of in public. You are to protect her, stand up for her, and have her back. She is a daughter of the King and deserves to be treated as such.

Lea and I married when we were very young. It seemed to be more acceptable back in the '80s. She had just turned eighteen when we got married. We had dated for four years and had talked about marriage a lot. The year before we got married, we started making plans ... future plans, wedding plans, and life plans. It was official.

The next summer after she turned eighteen and graduated from high school, we would marry and go off to school together.

I had already been living two hours away going to school for the last year, and we did not want to be apart any longer. I thought the plan was absolutely perfect until she said the following words that caused me to want to call the whole thing off: "Are you going to talk to my dad about all this?"

Her dad was a good man, but he was a little scary to me. I was young, and he was big. I was a little fearful of him because I wanted to be a good husband and not let him down. He would be my earthly father-in-law, and I had no doubt he would keep me accountable when it came to the way I treated his daughter. Not long after we married, it occurred to me that I had a heavenly Father-in-law that would also hold me accountable for the way I treated His daughter. He is a MUCH scarier father-in-law than my earthly one.

I will say this as clearly as I can, I believe God will hold a husband accountable for the way he treats his wife...HIS daughter. I tell you this so you don't stand before God someday and say, "I had no clue."

Think back to the first two people ever married, Adam and Eve. At first, Adam was all by himself;

Eve had yet to be created. *"The Lord God said, 'It is not good for the man to be alone.'" (Genesis 2:18)*

Our friends, Richard and JeannaLynn May, sum this verse up well. They say, "God knew what Adam needed and what he didn't. Adam was alone, and God didn't give him a buddy, a neighbor, a church or a service club. God gave him what he needed most, a wife."[2]

When Eve is finally created she is presented to Adam. Note verse 22, *"Then the Lord God made a woman from the rib he had taken out of the man, and he brought her to the man."* She belonged to God first, not Adam. God brought her to Adam, and presented her to him. It's as if someone said, "Who gives this bride?" and someone replied, "We do ... God the Father, God the Son and God the Holy Spirit."

Eve was God's before she was Adam's, just like your wife was God's before she became yours. She is not just a daughter of a king, she is a daughter of the King of Kings. Treat her as you would a princess because your heavenly Father-in-law is watching.

Another verse that makes this even more clear is 1 Peter 3:7. *"In the same way you husbands must live with your wives with the proper understanding that they are more delicate than you. Treat them with respect, because they also will receive, together with you, God's gift of life.* **Do this so that nothing will interfere with your prayers."** (GNT, emphasis ours)

Okay guys, notice several things here. First, she is more delicate than you. She is fragile. You are to treat her as such. Meaning, she is to be treated like she is a special, valuable gift that you do not want to break. Handle her gently.

Lea has a cabinet full of her favorite dishes. They are some we got for wedding gifts and some that our mothers gave to Lea before they passed. Usually at Thanksgiving or Christmas, when all the family is home, she will use these very special dishes. I know what they mean to her, so when she asks me to help set the table, I treat those dishes with the utmost care and gentleness. To damage one would break my heart because it would break her heart. I carefully move the dishes from the cabinet to the table while watching out for dogs underfoot, shoes I might trip over, or anything else that could get in my way. I usually don't do anything very slowly. Most of the time, I move at a high rate of speed, but when I move these dishes, I do it with extreme care.

This is the same concept that God expects us to have with our wives. We are to treat them gently in every area of marriage. We are to treat our wives with gentleness:

- Verbally

- Physically

- Emotionally

- Sexually

In every area, you should treat her like she is fine china because she is ... and because God said that is how you are to treat her. Did you notice the second part of 1 Peter 3:7 we put in bold? *"Do this so that nothing will interfere with your prayers."*

If you are unwilling to treat her gently, like a daughter of the King, then take note from this verse that God will not take your prayers into consideration. Your prayers will be *hindered*, as another translation puts it. I personally do not want anything to hinder my prayers. I want to know that when I pray and ask God to bless me and my family, He hears me and is willing to do what I ask. 1 Peter 3:7 is a sobering verse.

Several years ago, Lea and I took a trip with a couple. I picked up very quickly that one of his favorite things to do was "jokingly" criticize his wife and then laugh about it. He made left-handed compliments about her cooking, her looks, her clothes and on and on. He always finished with a big laugh, like it was funny.

I tried my best that weekend to set a positive example of how to treat your wife. I remember specifically commenting about how good our wives were, how pretty they were, and how much more fun it was that they were with us. Every time I made a positive comment, he would jokingly say something negative about his wife and then laugh.

When I finally realized he wasn't catching on, I leaned over where only he could hear me and said, "Hey, I don't want to make this awkward or put a damper on our weekend, but I've noticed you are always cutting down your wife and then laughing it off as a joke. I just want you to know that is not healthy for your marriage. Your wife will never be all you want her to be as a wife because you are always cutting her down and not building her up." I then said, "If you keep this up, there is a good chance she will either leave you, or she will find someone who treats her better." His response was simply something like, "Pssh, I am the best thing she's got going."

The rest of the weekend he toned it down, but it

didn't stop. About a year later, he showed up in my office for help. Any guesses what kind of help he needed? Yep, you guessed it. She had left him. "How do I get her back?" he asked. While I did say in a nice way, "I tried to warn you," I refrained from saying what I really wanted to say which was, "I guess you are no longer the best thing she's got going."

Husbands, you can't treat your wife like a doormat and expect her to be the wife you want her to be. She needs love, praise and gentleness ... lots of gentleness.

Lea and I have four sons, and I have worked hard to raise those four boys to treat their mother with the utmost respect and gentleness. I often joked with them when they were younger, "You are to always speak kindly to your mother and treat her well. I brought you into this world, and I can take you out of this world and create another just like you, if you don't."

My sons can still quote this phrase because they have heard it so many times. Although I was joking, they also knew I was serious. We have raised four young men who adore their mother and would do anything for her. As a father, I could not be prouder.

A few years ago, while taking our oldest son to the airport to catch a plane, we stopped off at a store because we had some time to spare before he needed to check in. As it got close to the time we had set to leave, I stressed a little bit about getting to the airport late. No matter how many times I told Lea, "We need to go," she seemed to not be in a hurry. In frustration, I finally raised my voice and used a tone that was not fit for a daughter of the King, and my oldest son who overheard it, looked across the aisle and sternly said, "No sir, we do not talk to her like that. You need to just chill out." He was spot on to correct his father, and I could not have been prouder of him that day. It was then I realized I had succeeded in teaching our sons to treat their mother with respect and gentleness.

If strangers, coworkers or even church friends see a better side of us than our spouse does, something is terribly wrong. No one wants to be married to a critic. Be your spouse's biggest fan, not their biggest critic.

The tongue has the power of life and death ...
(Proverbs 18:21, NIV)

5 – LET'S GET NAKED, BUT NOT THAT WAY

Warning: There is a chance that this chapter might make some of you mad. We are okay with that. There's also a really good chance this chapter might make you shake your head and think we are being silly or over dramatic. You might think we are making WAY too big of a deal out of things that aren't a big deal. We are simply pointing out things in this chapter that we see every day that cause marriages to struggle.

I imagine when Adam was naming all the animals, he was looking for one he could hang out with, a friend, a *suitable helper*, as referenced in the Bible. *"Now the Lord God had formed out of the ground all the wild animals and all the birds in the sky. He brought them to the man to see what he would name them; and whatever the man called each living creature, that was its name. So the man gave names to all the livestock, the birds in the sky and all the wild animals. But for Adam no suitable helper was found."* (Genesis 2:19-20, NIV)

Picture the scenario as animals were coming to him:

"You are a giraffe."

"You are a hippopotamus."

"You are a baboon."

"You are a brown cow."

Maybe he kept thinking sooner or later someone would show up in the line of animals that was like him. *"But for Adam, no suitable helper was found."*

"So the Lord God caused the man to fall into a deep sleep; and while he was sleeping, he took one of the man's ribs and then closed up the place with flesh. Then the Lord God made a woman from the rib he had taken out of the man, and he brought her to the man." (Genesis 2:21-22, NIV)

The Lord caused the man to fall into a deep sleep, (most men have no problem with that at all) and when he woke up ... boom ... there was Eve. Can you just imagine Adam's jaw dropping open? She was by far the most beautiful thing he had ever seen; definitely more beautiful than the old brown cow he had seen just before God knocked him out.

Don't you dare read this next text with no emotion because Adam is SO excited. *"The man said, 'This is now bone of my bones and flesh of my flesh; she shall be called woman, for she was taken out of man.'"* (vs. 23) I can see him saying that while grinning from ear to ear!

The text goes on to say, *"That is why a man leaves his father and mother and is united to his wife, and they become one flesh. Adam and his wife were both naked, and they felt no shame."* (vs. 24 & 25)

Take note of verse 25: *Adam and his wife were both naked.* The word naked here is very important because it means much more than they weren't wearing any clothes. The word naked here means "without covering." There was **nothing** covered from one another; there was nothing hidden from one another. They were totally naked with one another ... physically, emotionally, sexually and in every other area. They had absolutely nothing to hide.

God created marriage for a husband and a wife to be naked with one another - for there to be nothing hidden from one another - no secrets. Did you notice the last part of verse 25? When a husband and wife are naked with one another in every area of their marriage, there is no shame. That is how God intended marriage to be. Fast forward to today, where we have come a long way away from the garden. Marriages today struggle with secrecy, hidden text messages, and secret porn addictions. Because of these secrets, there IS shame.

Being naked with one another as a husband and wife is one of the greatest blessings you can give each other. When you choose to be naked emotionally, physically, spiritually, and in every other area, marriage works as it was originally designed.

When we allow Satan to enter in and deceive us, shame enters into our relationship, and we lose our "nakedness" with one another.

Cell Phones

Everyone has a cell phone these days. We feel they are a necessity. They have made our lives both better and worse. Lea and I are able to do good things with our cell phones. We can check in with one another, schedule and keep track of future speaking engagements and dates, communicate with our children, etc. Lots of good things can be done with a cell phone.

Cell phones can also be a great deterrent and stumbling block when it comes to marriage. I have a friend who is a district judge that hears lots of divorce cases. I asked him not long ago, "What are you seeing in the courtroom that we need to be talking about in our workshops?" He replied, "Trey, it is amazing. Probably 98% of the people that are getting a divorce have been having an emotional affair with someone they are not married to through texting."

We see it every day. Someone locks their phone with a passcode so their spouse can't see what they are doing and who they are texting. It has become one of the most dangerous things in marriage. It starts simply as a few texts to someone of the opposite sex that you are not married to, and before you know it, you are involved in a full-blown emotional affair that you are hiding from your spouse. Shame enters the relationship because "nakedness" has been lost.

A husband sat in my office not long ago and said, "My wife has locked me out of her cellphone, and she does not allow me to see it or use it anymore. Should I be worried?" I explained to him that those were red flag warning signs and suggested he check his cell phone bill to see if he recognized all of the numbers she was texting. I can still remember him saying, "I have a hard time believing she would be texting someone that I don't know about." He came back to my office three days later with his cell phone records. He had found a number that he didn't know, which she had texted over 2000 times the previous month. My heart broke for him as he had to confront her with what was going on.

Lea and I just recently broke down and bought new phones. They have face recognition as a security feature to unlock the phone. We set up our phones so that *both* of us can unlock *both* phones. I want her to know that she is welcome to pick up, look at, use, or browse through my history or anything on my phone any time she would like to do so. I have absolutely nothing to hide from her on my phone, and I want her to know that. My phone is her phone. She is free to use it anytime she wants. We have no secrets and nothing hidden from one another. That is how God intended marriage to be. Naked.

Without sounding preachy, let me throw this out there to you. You may think cheating on your spouse is flirting, touching, and having sex with someone of the opposite sex that you are not married to. I would like to tell you, if you are locking your spouse out of your cell phone, or deleting text messages because you are texting someone other than your spouse, you are not headed toward cheating, you are already there! Emotional affairs are real. Emotional affairs are cheating.

Lea and I text people of the opposite sex but only to pass on information like, "Don't forget the meeting at 6:00 tomorrow night." We do not text people of the opposite sex for personal reasons. Meaning, we do not text people we are not married to and ask things like "How was your day?" Those are things reserved for married couples, so we are cautious about our friendships of the opposite sex. We want to be totally naked with one another when it comes to our cell phones and electronics.

It doesn't matter what it is, if you are having to hide it from your spouse, you should not be doing it. In your marriage vows you promised to be faithful to your spouse. Cheating on your marriage can be done in many ways.

* **PHYSICALLY CHEATING** is when you are involved with someone sexually that is not your spouse. Some people call it an affair or sleeping around ... it's cheating. It is wrong. It's adultery, and there is NO excuse for this, ever.

* **EMOTIONAL CHEATING** is when you have made an unhealthy friendship with someone of the opposite sex. You have become attached to that person in a way that you should be with your spouse. You constantly text, talk or want to spend time together. You hide this relationship and the details of it from your spouse because deep down you know it is wrong. Emotional affairs are as dangerous and as wrong as physical ones.

* **MENTAL AFFAIRS** take place with pornography, soft-core porn, etc. We believe this is not okay behavior. It is a perverse and ridiculous intrusion into your relationship. It is an insult; it is disloyal; and it is cheating. Consider how use of pornography would make your partner feel. They would most likely feel ugly, hurt, deceived, lied to or inadequate. Mental affairs need to stop because they will erode your relationship.

Guard yourself from affairs of any kind. Don't try to justify them. They are wrong. Just in case someone is reading this and doesn't know, God will never bring you another person's spouse as an answer to your prayers. Your soulmate is not another person's spouse. Be faithful to the one you promised that you would be faithful to, and pursue them ... not others.

Friendships of the Opposite Sex

The majority of all affairs in marriage begin with the words, "We are just friends." Most all affairs take place with people we already know and are friends with. *"Adultery is a brainless act, soul-destroying, self-destructive ..."* (Proverbs 6:32, MSG)

Be extremely cautious with friendships of the opposite sex. If your spouse is uncomfortable with a friendship you have with someone of the opposite sex, listen to them. In a healthy marriage a mature person will cut off any person that threatens their marriage or relationship with their spouse.

We don't believe anyone ever goes looking to have an affair. Instead, affairs happen over time when we let our guard down and quit focusing on our marriage. One of the best things you can do to keep your marriage strong is to pay attention to the signs that your relationship is headed in the wrong direction. Here are some early warning signs you might be headed for an affair:

- You have an "It'll never happen to us" attitude. Don't EVER let your guard down. It can happen to anyone.

- You confide in someone of the opposite sex about your marriage problems. Go back and underline this one. If you are talking to someone of the opposite sex about issues you are having in your marriage, you are headed for BIG trouble.

- You neglect your marriage and no longer try to meet your spouse's needs.

- You are not doing regular check-ups with your spouse asking, "How are we doing?"

- You are not being proactive in the growth of your marriage.

- You focus all your energy and attention on your children and not your marriage.

- You are locking your phone from your spouse, or deleting texts or Facebook messages so your spouse won't see them.

- You find yourself dressing up and paying more attention to your appearance in hopes that "someone" will notice you.

- You are keeping secrets or hiding things from your spouse about a friendship you have with someone of the opposite sex.

You might not agree with that list. Some of it might

even make you angry, but we have seen those things lead to affairs time and time again. Marriage will be full of ups and downs. "For better and for worse" was part of your vows. Every marriage has better and every marriage has worse, but no matter how bad your marriage gets, there is never a reason or an excuse to cheat.

Social Media

Another area in which we need to be "naked" with our spouse is social media. A few short years ago, social media was not even a thing. Now we have the option of things like Facebook, Instagram, Twitter, SnapChat, etc., but we also know there needs to be some rules when it comes to social media and our marriage.

DON'T SPEND MORE TIME ON SOCIAL MEDIA THAN YOU SHOULD. Staying up at night on social media while your spouse goes to bed without you is probably not a good idea. How much time is too much time? That is a discussion to have with your spouse, but always make sure that you don't ignore the people in the room with you to focus on people on your phone. What I mean is, the people in the room with you are more important than the people you are social networking with, or texting with, on the phone/computer.

We heard a man say, "My favorite time of the night is when my wife's phone battery finally dies, because then she pays some attention to me." That totally broke our hearts. Here was a husband begging for some attention from his wife, and she was more interested in the things on her phone. We remember thinking, "Please Lord, don't ever let that be us. Help us to avoid that temptation."

NEVER HIDE THINGS FROM YOUR SPOUSE ON SOCIAL MEDIA. If you are hiding things from your spouse on social media, that is a sign that you are doing something you should not be doing. Whether it is messages, friendships, history, etc., don't lose the "nakedness" God designed for your marriage.

SHARE YOUR PASSWORD WITH YOUR SPOUSE. Personally, we share every password we have. I make sure Lea knows what my passwords are because generally there is a good chance I am going to forget them. ☺ Seriously, we want one another to know that we are welcome to use or look at each other's social media at any time. Some couples share the same social media account, which is also a good idea. Personally, I am much more active on social media than Lea, so sharing the same account would drive her crazy.

Whatever works best for your marriage, be very diligent to be open, honest, and transparent with your social media accounts. Hiding passwords from your spouse is like putting a passcode on your phone and not allowing your spouse to access it. It throws up red flags everywhere.

NEVER ACCEPT A FRIEND REQUEST FROM ANYONE OF THE OPPOSITE SEX ON SOCIAL MEDIA THAT YOUR SPOUSE IS UNCOMFORTABLE WITH. Befriending an old boyfriend, girlfriend or Ex should NEVER be done without fully discussing it with your spouse. Your spouse should be your best friend. They should be the most important person in your world. Their friendship should matter more than a friendship on Facebook.

We once knew a man who befriended his old high school girlfriend on Facebook. It seemed pretty innocent at the time. She told him that she was going through a divorce and needed someone to talk to. After several months of long conversations on Facebook Messenger, he came to us and said, "Old feelings have come back for my high school sweetheart, and I think I married the wrong person. I am not sure anymore what to do." This was a husband and father of four who had been happily married for over fourteen years. Of course, all of these messages and the friendship had been kept from his wife. After some long talks and counseling, he made the right decision. He told his old high school sweetheart that he could no longer visit with her, or even be friends on Facebook, and then he did the right thing by blocking her to avoid any future temptations.

Be cautious about social media and relationships you have had in the past. Facebook is not the place to look up your old boyfriend/girlfriend or Ex of any kind.

UNFRIEND ANYONE WHO CROSSES NORMAL BOUNDARIES. Interestingly enough, Mark Zuckerberg can thank William Shakespeare for first using the word "unfriend" as a verb in the 17th century.[1] In recent years, it has become a commonly used word in the 21st century, and it is an important word when it comes to social media and your marriage. Listen to the little voice in your head. If something tells you "This isn't right," then it probably isn't. If someone seems too friendly, or flirty, you need to rethink that social media friendship.

POST PICTURES. Post pictures of you AND your spouse on social media, or use a picture of the two of you together as your profile picture. We have noticed on Facebook and Instagram the difference between husbands and wives. Wives will have seven million pictures of their kids. (Okay, that might be a little bit of an exaggeration, but not much.) You can scroll through their timeline or photos, and it is kid picture after kid picture. Husbands, on the other hand, will have dozens of pictures of their truck, their dog, their hunting trip, their fishing excursion, or their favorite sports team, etc.

It has been said that you can tell a lot about a person's passions by looking at their social media page. If someone looked at yours, what would they think you are passionate about? It is okay to be passionate about your kids, your hobbies, or your favorite sports team, but don't be ashamed to let the world know you are madly and passionately in love with your spouse. Post pictures of you two together on a regular basis. It's a healthy thing to do.

DON'T BE AFRAID TO PROCLAIM YOUR LOVE FOR YOUR SPOUSE ON SOCAL MEDIA. Someone of the opposite sex won't question your love for your spouse, if you regularly brag on your spouse. It does not hurt to tell the world, "I married the most beautiful woman in the world," or "I married the most handsome man in the world."

Praising your spouse on social media is a very healthy thing to do. Our friend, Haley, is very good at this. Once or twice a month she writes on Facebook about how awesome her husband Randy is. Randy will pretend like he doesn't like it, but he actually loves it, and we love the way that Randy treats Haley like a queen. We think that might have a lot to do with the fact that she is so good at praising him.

INSTANT MARRIAGE BOOST:

Change your social media profile picture to one of you and your spouse together; then post something about why you love them.

NEVER USE YOUR STATUS OR POST TO COMPLAIN ABOUT YOUR SPOUSE. Okay people, here is one you need to underline or highlight. This is a no-no! There is never a time or place on any social media for you to air your grievances to the world about your spouse. The very best person to talk to about problems you are having with your spouse is your spouse. I reminded a friend of mine recently who was saying negative things about his wife on Facebook,

"Speaking negatively about your wife for the world to read, will never improve your marriage. It will only hurt it." Praise your spouse for others to hear; don't publicly criticize them. Some of us need to take the old advice, "If you don't have anything nice to say, don't say anything at all."

THINK BEFORE YOU TYPE. This is going to sound silly, but hear us out. Don't make comments that come across as flirty or suggestive. Be cautious about how you praise people of the opposite sex on social media. If someone gets a promotion at work, by all means praise them and wish them well. If someone posts a picture of themself all dressed up for a party, it is not a good idea for you to say, "Wow, you look smoking hot!" Comments like that should be reserved for your spouse, not for someone of the opposite sex on social media.

We even take it a step further in our own marriage. We are cautious about clicking the "Like" button on a picture of someone of the opposite sex. Several years ago, my niece posted several pictures of herself on Instagram having a great time at the lake. She was dressed in a swimsuit that was appropriate for a teenager, but I was cautious not to "Like" those pictures. Not because I don't love my niece, but because I did not want anyone else to see that I had liked those pictures and think, "I don't know who the girl in the bikini is, but Trey sure likes her pictures." I do not want anyone to think that I am not 100% committed to my wife. You may think this is taking things too far, but in this day and time, it's probably not.

No matter how many friends and followers you have on social media, remember that your #1 friend should be your spouse. Strive to better that relationship on a daily basis. Work 1000 times harder to grow in your marriage relationship than you do at growing followers on social media. The last thing you want is thousands of followers, while the love between you and your best friend slowly dies out.

Honesty Builds Intimacy and Trust

We have talked a lot about not hiding things from your spouse that deal with social media, pornography, or friendships with the opposite sex, but quite frankly, nothing should be hidden from your spouse - no matter how small it is. Maybe your husband notices your new pair of shoes and says, "I didn't think we had money in the budget right now for new shoes." You reply, "These shoes aren't new. I've had them forever," but you really bought them two days ago. Maybe your wife smells smoke on you and says, "You promised you were going to quit smoking!" You slipped and had a cigarette, but instead of coming clean, you tell her you went to a very smoky restaurant at lunch. Hiding something, whether big or small, from your spouse because you want to avoid trouble or keep the peace is dishonesty and can destroy trust in marriage.

Some people keep things from their spouse that would cause them to worry, like trouble at work or financial stress. They truly feel they are protecting their spouse from worry, stress, or harm, but this is still dishonesty. It is not being totally "naked" or "uncovered" in marriage as God intended. There are many verses in God's word that tell us how He feels about dishonesty. Proverbs 12:22 says, *"The Lord detests lying lips, but he delights in those who tell the truth."* (NLT) God wants us to be honest in all things. Any form of dishonesty in marriage can damage intimacy and trust.

Dishonesty, secrets, hiding things, and friendships of the opposite sex can often be marriage killers. Due to the times we now live in with cell phones and social media, we are dealing with new challenges and temptations today that we did not have ten years ago. Work hard to be uncovered and naked in every area of your marriage.

Back to Adam and Eve ... you know the story.
After Adam and Eve sinned, they immediately
"covered" themselves with fig leaves. In marriage,
when sin enters, the first thing we do is try to
"cover" ourselves, and "nakedness" no longer
exists. Protect the trust and the nakedness in your
marriage. Trust is a foundation piece of your
marriage. If you have it, protect it with all your
might because once you have lost it, it is
extremely hard to get back.

**Adam and his wife were both naked, and they
felt no shame.**

(Genesis 2:25)

6 – LET'S GET NAKED, YES THAT WAY!

Every spring I teach a series of lessons on marriage at the church where I preach. I have done this for as long as I can remember. About twelve years ago when I sat down to plan out my spring preaching schedule, I decided I would like to do a lesson on sex. It is a biblical topic, but no one seems to be preaching about it. I wanted to talk about God's view of sex and how He created it as a gift for marriage. I approached my church leadership and asked for their wisdom and permission. They were in full agreement that it was something everyone needed to hear. When the week rolled around for the "sex sermon," I was a bit nervous. I had no doubt that in the hundred-year history of that congregation, there had never been a sermon on the topic of sex. I knew this was going to get people out of their comfort zone, including me.

On Thursday of that week, I got a call from the man who would be leading our singing that upcoming Sunday. He was an older man and didn't know what he was about to get himself into. When I saw on my caller ID who it was, I became a little anxious because I knew why he was calling.

I picked up the phone and said "Hello." He replied with, "I am checking in to see what the sermon topic is this Sunday, so I can pick out some songs that go along with it." I told him that the sermon this week would be on the topic of sex. There was silence on the other end of the phone for a solid ten to fifteen seconds. It reached the point that I was just about to ask, "Are you still there?" when he finally replied. He said, "I'll do my best to come up with some songs," and quickly hung up. I wondered what songs he would come up with that would fit the topic of sex. I have sung just about every song in our church songbook and felt certain none were going to fit.

Sunday finally rolled around. Everyone had read in the bulletin and seen in the handout what the sermon topic was for that morning. When the song leader got up to start the service, he simply said "I have looked for songs to fit this week's topic, but I have found none. Does anyone know of a song that might fit with the topic today?"

From the back, an older gentleman raised his hand and quietly said, "How about *Precious Memories*?" Okay, don't put much stock in that last part, but had it really happened, it would have made a great story!

Sex is not a topic that Christians or the church talk about much. Everyone else talks about it. Songs on the radio sing about it. Books tell stories about it. Movies talk about it and sometimes portray it. We even see it on billboards and in commercials. It seems like everyone is talking about it except for the people who actually need to talk about it.

Churches need to talk about sex; parents need to talk to their kids about sex; and Christians need to talk about sex. If the only thing Christian kids ever hear about sex is "Don't do it," we are failing them miserably. God talks about sex. He is the creator of sex. He created it and called it good. It is time we quit shying away from the subject that everyone else in the world wants to talk about. Someone needs to tell the correct side of the story when it comes to sex and God's plan for it.

It all began in the garden in Genesis 2. It was Adam and Eve's wedding day. Genesis 2:24 says, *"That is why a man leaves his father and mother and is united to his wife, and they become one flesh."* (NIV) Adam was so excited to see Eve that he wrote a poem. Men do not write poems unless they are sickly in love. *"Bone of my bone, and flesh of my flesh,"* Adam said. He was awestruck at her beauty, and get this, God wasn't offended. God knew what was going to happen between them ... He had just given Adam a naked wife. God wasn't bothered by them having sex, and He isn't bothered by you having sex. He is bothered when we use it in ways He never intended.

Adam and Eve had a unique marriage. Neither of them had the opportunity to learn about marriage from a parent. What they did learn was probably taught to them by God, or they learned things the hard way.

One of the things that we can learn from the first marriage is that God created our spouse to be our standard of beauty. Adam and Eve were one another's standard for beauty. Adam believed with all his heart that Eve was the most beautiful woman in the world. Eve had no doubt that Adam was the most handsome man in the world. Of course, they were the only people in the world, but don't miss the point. They were one another's standard of beauty.

We believe that is what God intended for marriage. You should see your spouse as the most beautiful or most handsome person in the world. No one compares to them. Your spouse is your standard of beauty. Whether you have been married for three months, thirteen years or thirty years, no one should compare to your spouse. Whether their hair is turning gray or turning loose, your spouse should be the most attractive person in the world in your eyes. Your spouse is the only person you should have eyes for.

We are bothered by married people who drool over other people. Whether you want to call it eye-candy or something else, it can cause your spouse to feel as if they don't quite measure up, or that you wish they looked more like the sports star, actor, singer, or model that you are going on and on about. If an attractive person walks by you and your spouse, it is not wise to let your eyes follow. Pursue what you have; let your spouse know there is no one that is more attractive to you than they are.

Sex Is A god

Sex was created by God to be a gift to married

people. It is as if God shows up at the wedding reception and says, "I have a great wedding gift for you. Enjoy!" God never created sex to be shameful or dirty. If it has become bad, it's because we have messed it up in the world. We have made it something it was not supposed to be.

The world has made sex a god. Meaning, whatever you obsess about becomes your idol. We are not supposed to put anything above God, yet the world has made a god out of sex. Every song, movie, magazine, and TV commercial these days is sexually oriented. Sex has become a common theme in our world, and sadly the world has it all wrong.

Sex sells, and everyone knows it. Commercials that have absolutely nothing to do with sex or romance use both to sell their products. There are hamburger commercials with girls in bikinis. There is probably someone in this world that thinks you get one of those in the happy meal box along with the burger. We hate to break it to you, but you also won't look like those girls in bikinis by eating hamburgers.

We saw a commercial recently for microwave rice. We are not sure why anyone would use sex to sell microwave rice, but this company did. We found it humorous and silly. A man and woman come home from the grocery store and place all their bags on the counter. The man reaches into one of the grocery bags and pulls out a package of microwave rice. He then puts the rice into the microwave and sets it for one minute. As he does this, the lights in the kitchen dim and romantic music starts to play. The microwave goes "ding," and the man retrieves the bag of rice. By this time, the woman in the commercial has found her way over to the man and is looking lustfully at the bag of rice. As he opens the top of the bag, steam comes out. Get this, he reaches over and grabs a plastic fork. I'm not sure why he chose a plastic fork, but I guess there is something sexy about plastic forks. He takes a plastic fork, scoops up a small bite of rice and feeds it to the woman. The look on her face is ecstasy as she tastes the rice in her mouth. The commercial closes with the words, "You're going to want some of this." It's ridiculous that sex can be used to sell microwave rice. Who knows, maybe somewhere out there is a guy named Bubba watching the commercial thinking to himself, "I've gotta get me some of that rice. Me and my wife are gonna have a date in the kitchen tonight." (We realize we have just offended everyone by the name of Bubba. We apologize. ☐)

Sex was not created to be an idol. It was never

created to be a god. Did you know that the porn industry's net worth is approximately $97 billion? That is billion with a B, not million. Just to help you get a grasp on what $97 billion is, the porn industry makes more money than Major League Baseball, the NFL, and the NBA combined.[1] If anything, this should tell us that the world has made sex a god.

Sex Is Gross

Often times when churches, Christians and parents see how the world has messed up what God created as beautiful, we overreact. We tend to swing the pendulum too far the other direction, and we teach sex to our youth as gross, dirty, or shameful. God never intended sex to be any of those things.

Sometimes we choose to just not talk about it at all ... if we ignore the subject, it will just go away. We were raised in homes much like that. Sex was never a topic, was never really discussed, and if it came on television, someone was supposed to get up and turn it off. We still laugh today that it made for an awkward honeymoon night. It was a night that was to be beautiful and perfect, but we remember vividly telling each other that we were a little embarrassed that everyone knew what we were doing! □

Talking to your kids about sex is a healthy and necessary thing to do. If you wait until they are in junior high, you have waited too long because they start hearing things in elementary school (and probably all wrong). Start with a few simple basics, and you can make it a regular topic as they grow older and need to know more. There are good books available that help guide you through age appropriate discussions you can have with your children. They need to know that sex was not created to be dirty or shameful; it was created as a beautiful gift from God to married people.

Sex Is a Gift

Let's discuss some different ways that God created sex as a gift.

- Sex is for pleasure. God created sex for you to enjoy with your spouse. It is when two people become one. Sexual intimacy is what separates roommates from soulmates. There is no connection in this world as powerful as the connection of sex in marriage. While most of the creatures God created in this world only have sex for procreation, God allows us to have sex for pleasure. He is a good God.

- *Sex is for procreation.* The first time sex is actually mentioned in the Bible is in the fourth chapter of Genesis. Sex was going on long before then, but it is specifically mentioned here because the first example of procreation is going to take place. *"Adam made love to his wife Eve, and she became pregnant and gave birth to Cain."* (Genesis 4:1, NIV) According to Google, there are 360,000 children born every day. I think we have this procreation thing down in our world.

- *Sex is knowledge.* In the translation of the verse mentioned above, it says, *"Adam made love to his wife Eve"*, but the old King James Version says, *"And Adam knew his wife Eve ..."* The Hebrew word used here is *yada'*, which means "to know." It is the same word David used in the Psalms, "You have searched me, Lord, and you know me." (Psalms 139:1, NIV) Believe it or not, the word "know" is actually a really great translation for the word sex because sex is knowledge. Sexual intimacy provides an avenue to get to know someone better than anyone else in the world knows them. Lea and I know one another better than anyone else knows us in the entire world, and much of that is due to the intimacy that God created in sex. Your knowledge of your spouse goes far beyond what others know of your spouse because sex is about knowledge and knowing one another in an intimate way.

- Sex is for protection from temptation. We personally believe a good healthy sex life is a great deterrent to temptation. We are not the only ones who think this. In I Corinthians 7:3-6 Paul said this, *"The husband should fulfill his wife's sexual needs, and the wife should fulfill her husband's needs. The wife gives authority over her body to her husband, and the husband gives authority over his body to his wife. Do not deprive each other of sexual relations, unless you both agree to refrain from sexual intimacy for a limited time so you can give yourselves more completely to prayer. Afterward, you should come together again so that Satan won't be able to tempt you because of your lack of self-control."* (NLT) Did you catch that last part? *"Come together again so that Satan won't be able to tempt you."* There is protection from temptation when you have sex with your spouse. That does not mean you will never be tempted or that you won't give in to temptation just because you are having sex in your marriage, but it provides a level of protection.

- Sex is for comfort. Sex can be used to comfort yourself or your spouse. After a particularly rotten day, a silly argument, during a time of grief, or

maybe just one of those days when nothing seems to go your way, comfort sex is a real thing. In 2 Samuel 12, we are told that David and Bathsheba lost their baby and came together sexually to comfort one another.

- Sex is for oneness. *"And the two shall become one flesh."* (Genesis 2:24, NKJV) Oneness is an amazing concept. The fact that two people can become one is miraculous. Two people get to know one another emotionally, mentally, spiritually, physically (i.e. attraction), and then sexually. That is God's plan for relationships.

There is amazing power in sex. It is like a glue that bonds a couple together. The world has tried to make sex common, but God made it special. Did you know there is a hormone that is released in the human body called oxytocin? Oxytocin is a bonding hormone. Oxytocin is released into a woman's body when a baby is born. That hormone races through a mother's body and helps her to bond with, or "claim", that child. God made the human body to work this way so mothers would say, "That is my child." Another time when oxytocin is released into the body is when a mother breast-feeds a child. Again, this is God's way of helping a mother claim that child as hers.

Another occasion oxytocin is released into the

body is when a husband and wife have sex. Both feel connected to one another through the act of sex. It is God's way of bonding people and making them one. Oxytocin is a powerful thing. As silly as it may sound, we notice ourselves getting on one another's nerves, at each other's throats, and not liking each other very well when we find ourselves going for a long period of time without sexual intimacy. We become somewhat disconnected with one another. Once we come together sexually, it's as if a switch has been flipped, and we like each other and feel close again. We get along much better and feel connected again.

We used to have cordless phones in our house. If we let them go too long without reconnecting to the base, they wouldn't work. Sometimes we would try to answer a phone call and get nothing. We could simply run into the kitchen, connect the phone to the base for a minute, pick it back up, and it would work fine. The receiver needed to reconnect with the base in order to work as it was supposed to. That is the same way sex works in marriage. While it certainly isn't a cure all, it often helps to reconnect a couple. Sex between a husband and a wife is a beautiful gift from God.

Men vs. Women

God wired men and women up very different when it comes to sex. Husbands have the higher sexual drive in about 80% of marriages.[2] In fact, someone suggested we should have titled all of our chapters "Let's Get Naked" if we wanted men to read this book. Men generally have a high sex drive, and it only drops off on the day they die. (You were supposed to laugh at that.) This is not always the case, but generally it is.

Another difference is that most women reach a peak in their sex drive in their forties, which levels off after a few years. If you, as a woman, have a higher sex drive than your husband, don't think there is anything wrong with you or him. Sometimes it just works that way. If this has become an issue in your marriage, there is some great material on the topic of women having the higher sex drive listed in the end notes for this chapter.

Men and women are also very different in how quickly they get aroused. Men get aroused very quickly, while women can take much longer. We like to put it this way: men are like microwaves, and women are like slow cookers. You can heat up a cup of coffee in the microwave in about a minute. It only takes about one minute for a cup of coffee to go from being room temperature to hot. That is pretty much how most men are. They can go from being room temperature to extremely hot in about one minute.

Women, on the other hand, are more like a slow cooker. You must turn on the slow cooker early in the day in order to have food ready for supper. I cook in a slow cooker quite often. The first time Trey saw me cooking in the slow cooker, he was a little confused. It was eight o'clock in the morning, and we were fixing coffee. I started putting chicken, cream of mushroom soup and other things in my slow cooker. He asked, "Is that for breakfast?" To be fair, eight o'clock in the morning is not the usual time for people to cook supper, so I explained that slow cookers require eight to ten hours of cooking time. That is how slow cookers work.

Women are not microwave ovens; they do not heat up in one minute. They can't go from folding laundry and changing diapers to a sex goddess in a matter of seconds. Instead, they are more like slow cookers, which need to "cook" all day long in order to be prepared for sex.

Husbands need to understand that if you are waiting until bedtime to start "sowing the seeds of love," you might be starting too late. You need to start early in the day and continue to do little things for her throughout the day. Drop by her office with her favorite drink. Send her a message randomly during the day telling her you are thinking about her or that you appreciate her. Offer to help with supper or clean up the kitchen. These are just examples of things you can do all day long to bless your wife.

Wives, you may be thinking he is only doing these things because he wants sex. Whether that is the case or not, your husband wants you and is attracted to you sexually. That is a great and honorable thing.

Husbands, you also need to understand that what works to turn on your wife one time, might not work at all the next time. A woman's largest sexual organ is found in her mind, and minds are very complex. I wish there was a special formula that worked every time, but there just isn't. What I can guarantee though, is that she needs to feel an emotional connection from you before she is ready for a physical one. That's the reason you need to plug in the slow cooker early in the day.

Whether you are the husband or the wife, don't meet your spouse's sexual needs like it's a chore or a duty that you have to check off your list. No one wants their needs met out of obligation. Do your best to meet your spouse's needs with a good attitude, whatever those needs are. Often the person with the lower sex drive dictates how often sex takes place. Choose to meet in the middle with your spouse.

Intimacy Killers

It is important that you protect and guard the intimacy in your marriage. Do not allow things to crowd out or take priority over sex. You will never find time for sex; you must make time. Dr. Kevin Leman in his amazing book, *Sheet Music,* has a chapter called "Sex's Greatest Enemy." When we first got this book, that chapter title stood out to us. We were curious about what it was that was the greatest enemy of sex, so we flipped right over to that chapter. After reading a few lines into the chapter, we realized he believes the biggest enemy of sex *for women* is busyness or weariness, and we totally agree.[3]

Sometimes we get too busy with schedules that we find ourselves dropping in bed at night absolutely exhausted. We have no energy or desire for our spouse because we have nothing left at the end of a busy day.

If that is the case in your marriage, it is essential that you reprioritize your schedule. Learn to say "No" to some activities; make sure your calendar isn't so full that you're struggling to get it all done; but whatever you do, don't allow your relationship with your spouse to go from being soulmates to just roommates. Aim to give your best to your spouse, and not just your leftovers at the end of the day.

INSTANT MARRIAGE BOOST:

If you often find you are too tired for sex, think of your schedule right now and consider some ways to adjust it so that this is no longer the case.

Here are a few intimacy killers that are likely to sabotage your sex life:

- Allowing your children to sleep in the bed with you can sabotage your sex life. It's one thing if your child shows up in your bed at three o'clock in the morning because they were afraid. It is a different story if every night at nine o'clock they are going to sleep in your bed. Allowing your kids to sleep in your bed every night is a deterrent to intimacy. Make sure you work to keep your bed child free when at all possible.

We met a young couple at a workshop not long

ago who said they were struggling with intimacy because they had three small children sleeping in the bed with them every night. Talk about a bed full of people! They asked if we had any suggestions on how to fix that. Our suggestion for a situation like this is after the kids fall asleep, pick them up and carry them to their own beds. If all else fails, you move to one of their beds. When our children were small, we would lay down by them in their own bed for a few minutes until they fell asleep or got settled. Now granted, Trey would always fall asleep as well - he has the super power to fall asleep as soon as his head hits a pillow - so I would have to wake him before I went to bed, but we worked hard to keep kids out of our bed.

- Not making privacy a priority is a deterrent to sexual intimacy. We strongly believe that every master bedroom door should have a lock on it. If you are a contractor that builds houses, and you are currently reading this chapter, never build another house without a lock on the master bedroom door. It is a must. If you do not have a lock on your door, make it your goal this week to put one on. It is really hard to prepare your mind for sex knowing that at any moment a child might burst into your room. There is a bit more peace of mind when you know the door is locked.

We have had small children, so we understand what it's like putting multiple children to bed at night. It is a lot like the game, whack-a-mole; just about the time you think you got one down, another one pops up! When you finally get them all to bed, there is some peace of mind knowing that the door is locked, in case one decides to pop up again. Of course, things change when you get teenagers. We have learned you can't put teenagers to bed at 8:30, like you did when they were little, hoping to have some "alone time" with your spouse.

The best thing you can do at this stage in your life is to look across the room at your spouse, make eye contact, and say, "We are exhausted. We are headed to bed. Please turn all the lights out before you go to bed." Then both of you go to your room and lock the door behind you. Do what you can to make privacy a priority in your marriage.

- Another way couples sabotage their sex life is by letting themselves go. It is important to take care of your body and be the healthiest version of yourself as possible. You may have some physical issues that you need to talk to your doctor about. You may have some sexual issues in your past that you need to talk to a counselor about.

One common problem is low testosterone in middle aged men, which can cause some to struggle with erectile disfunction. There are a number of physical issues that can make sex difficult for women. Never let your pride get in the way of seeing a doctor or counselor. Be willing to do everything possible physically and mentally to make your sexual intimacy the best it can be.

- Some couples sabotage their intimacy when they quit flirting and having fun together.
Flirting is a healthy thing for your marriage. Flirting is something you did pre-marriage, and it should be part of your marriage still. You may not be newlyweds anymore, but that does not mean you can't still act like it.

- Many couples sabotage their sex life by saying "no" to sex more than they say "yes."
Sometimes the spouse with the stronger sex drive can feel like they are begging if they are always the one initiating sex. No one wants to feel like they have to beg for sex, or any of their needs to be met. Work hard to say "Yes," and even initiate sex, more than you say "No."

- A lack of communication can be a deterrent to sexual intimacy. If God is pro sex and the creator of sex, then He is okay with you talking about it. Talk about the things you like, as well as the things you're not crazy about. The best way to get what you want sexually from your spouse is to communicate. Don't be afraid to talk about sex. If this is an issue that you're a little uncomfortable with, we encourage you to read the book *Sheet Music: Uncovering the Secrets of Sexual Intimacy in Marriage* by Dr. Kevin Leman that we mentioned earlier. If you will underline things that are important to you and talk about the chapters as you go, you will be more comfortable communicating about sex by the time you get to the end of the book.

- Don't make everything more important than sex. As we said earlier, we tend to find ourselves pushing sex to the back burner in order to take care of everything else on the schedule. Make sure you have some energy left at the end of the day for your spouse, or even try starting your day with sex.

Some couples are uncomfortable scheduling sex. They say it takes the spontaneity out of it, and that scheduled sex is no fun, but sometimes scheduling it is a necessary thing. Scheduled sex is better than no sex. Since sex is a very mental thing for women, scheduling it can also be very beneficial. It allows you to prepare your mind and helps put you in the mood. We have also discovered that husbands tend to be more helpful, affectionate, and romantic on days that are circled on the calendar.

- ***Don't get stuck in a rut.*** Sexually, you don't have to always do the same thing the same way. You might try making love somewhere other than the bedroom. Try different positions and leaving the lights on. Some couples find that morning or afternoon sex is much better for them. There should never be such a thing as boring sex in marriage. Christian sex does not mean missionary position with the lights out, completely under the covers and done in 3 minutes. (Yes, we really just said that.) Have some fun with it.

- ***You will sabotage your sexual intimacy if you make it all about you.*** You may be the one with a higher sex drive that needs sex more often than your spouse, but if you make it all about you and not enjoyable for your spouse, things will deteriorate quickly. Sex should be *mutually satisfying*, so work hard to make sure your spouse enjoys sex as well. Communicate about their likes and dislikes, and figure out how to rock their world. If you want some good advice, ask them what "rocks their world."

God Is Not Ashamed of Sex

We had a couple in their nineties attend one of our workshops not long ago. They came dressed in their Sunday clothes and sat on the second row from the front. We found out they had been married over seventy years. They had come to our workshop to encourage all the younger couples there. They wanted others to know that if they could make it over seventy years, anyone could. We felt like we should have given them the microphones and let them teach the conference. They probably had forgotten more about marriage than we will ever know. We enjoyed the opportunity to get to visit with them between sessions.

When we came to our closing session on sex and intimacy, we wondered what this ninety-year old couple would have to say when we finished. After it was over the husband came up and said to Trey, "Do you want to know how I figured out that I was officially old?" Trey said he would love to know, and the older gentleman said with a smile, "Recently my wife asked me if I wanted to go upstairs and have sex. All I could tell her was that she was going to have to pick one of the two, because I did not have the energy to do both today." □ We loved meeting this couple who were proud of their marriage, were not afraid to talk about sex, and knew how to use a little humor.

God has never been afraid or embarrassed to talk about sex. The Bible is full of verses, chapters, and books that deal with sex. Proverbs 5:19 says *"Your wife is a lovely deer, a graceful doe. Let her breasts fill you at all times with delight; be intoxicated always in her love."* (ESV)

Wow, talk about PG-13 there! A lady once asked us, "Does God know they put that in His Bible?" Yes, He put it there, and He is unashamed by the sex He created and the way He created it.

When Solomon wrote the verse above, he was talking about more than just breasts. The last part of that verse talks about being intoxicated by your wife's love, drunk on sexual intimacy. May you never get full of your wife sexually and every other way. No matter how long you have been married, may you always crave her, never tiring of love.

God also chose to add the book of Song of Songs to His Word. It has eight chapters that drip with sex and intimacy. It is about a husband and a wife who seek each other out sexually. Each pursuing one another inside and outside the bedroom. It is a fabulous book that we don't spend enough time talking about. When you read the book from a modern translation, with an open mind, you often have to ask yourself, "Are they saying what I think they are saying they want to do?" The answer is yes.

"You are slender like a palm tree, and your breasts are like its clusters of fruit. I said, '"I will climb the palm tree and take hold of its fruit."'

(Song of Songs 7:7-8, NLT) The husband is clearly pursuing his wife. As you can see from this verse, God is not ashamed of sex. It is a beautiful gift He's given to married couples.

Husbands, when you read the Song of Songs, you will be fascinated with how much the woman also pursues her husband. She wants him sexually as much as he wants her. Often times men see this and say, "I want that. I want her to want me as much as I want her." If you read the entire book of the Song of Songs, you will also see that her husband treats her like a queen. He is delicate with her physically, emotionally and sexually. He refers to her as "darling" and other sweet words. We think it proves that if you will learn to treat your wife like a queen, the way God intended you to do, getting lucky won't require any real luck at all.

A Few Thoughts for Wives

If sexual fulfillment is more important to your husband than it is to you, make sure that you are willing to initiate occasionally when it comes to sex. What you don't want is for him to feel like he's having to beg, as we stated earlier. We already discussed how busy schedules and weariness is the biggest enemy of sex for women, but this is usually not the case for men. They can go from being sound asleep to fully aroused in less than a minute. Dr. Kevin Leman states that if a man doesn't feel pursued or wanted, he loses interest. Your husband wants to be needed, wanted, and prized. This requires time, energy, and foresight, but a man that is loved in a fulfilling way, will do anything for you. If a man feels loved and prized, he will knock down walls for you.[4]

If you are in the mood sexually, let him know. It is the perfect time to initiate it. You might be asking yourself, "How do I know if he is in the mood at that time?" Remember, he is a microwave. Just look at him, and if you see that he is still breathing, he is either in the mood or will be in about one minute.

Another good reason to initiate sex is because it makes your husband feel desired. If he is always the one doing the initiating and asking, that can be a bit frustrating, and make him feel undesirable. Just know your husband loves having you involved.

As we stated previously in this chapter, 80% of husbands have a higher sex drive than their wife. What this also means is that 20% of women have a higher sex drive than their husband. Women that fall into this percentage often despair and think there must be something wrong with them because their husband just does not seem interested in them sexually. Don't be hard on yourself. There is absolutely nothing wrong with you!

How to Turn on Your Wife ... A Few Tips for Men

A few years ago, we were invited to dinner at the home of some friends who had just built a new house. We were excited to see their house, and they were happy to give us a tour. Everything looked amazing. Toward the end of the tour was the kitchen. One of the things Ray was most excited about showing us was the giant pantry. He opened the doors to the pantry and said, "Look at the size of this thing. My wife loves having all this room."

One of the things I noticed on the top shelf of the pantry were several boxes of pumpkin spice coffee. We like pumpkin spice coffee on occasion, but this was a lot. In fact, it was several months' worth. I made a passing comment to Ray and Dondi, "You guys must sure love pumpkin spice coffee."

I knew immediately that I had struck a nerve because Ray ducked his head, and his wife immediately shook her head as if someone had done something wrong. Of course, I had to follow-up. I said, "So what's up with the pumpkin spice coffee?" Ray looked embarrassed and his wife said, "Tell them what you did, Ray." He mentioned something about being too embarrassed to tell the story, so finally Dondi spoke up and said, "Ray heard that pumpkin spice coffee was an aphrodisiac, so he bought several cases for me to drink."

At that point Ray raised his head and said with a smile, "And now because I blew the budget on pumpkin spice coffee, I can't get her to drink any of it." We spent the rest of the evening laughing and teasing Ray for believing that pumpkin spice coffee was an aphrodisiac.

Occasionally I still point out to Lea when we are at a coffee shop that they have pumpkin spice coffee. I'll ask her, with a smile on my face, "Can I get you an extra-large cup of that?"

Now before you go out and buy a bunch of pumpkin spice coffee and microwave rice, please know those things probably won't do the trick. Here are a few things your wife would absolutely love that work better than pumpkin spice coffee or microwave rice.

- Offer a "no strings attached" back-rub.
- Cook her supper and clean up.
- Buy her a gift certificate for a manicure/pedicure for no reason.
- Help clean the house.
- Do a chore for her she doesn't like to do.
- Surprise her with her favorite candy or drink.
- Send her some flowers at work.
- Call or text during the day just to tell her you are thinking about her.
- Line out a babysitter and take your wife on a date.
- Complement her every day.
- Hold her hand a lot.
- Offer to stay with the kids so she can get out of the house for a while.
- Keep the kids quiet on Saturday morning so she can sleep in.

These are all things most every wife loves. These are all "slow cooker" suggestions that you can do long before you start trying to sow the seeds of love in the bedroom. After seeing this long list of ways to turn on a wife, some women want a list of ways to turn on their husband? Simply put, no list is needed ... just show up naked! ☺

It takes more than sex to make a great marriage, but it is nearly impossible to build a great marriage without it!

~Dave Willis

7 – TREAT YOUR SPOUSE BETTER THAN THEY DESERVE

Have you ever thought to yourself that you married someone very different than you? Isn't it crazy how husbands and wives can be so different in marriage? The saying "opposites attract" must be true because we are two very different people. Sometimes it seems like we have more differences than we do similarities. For example, Lea insists that the toilet paper goes OVER the top of the roll, while Trey couldn't care less which direction the toilet paper goes as long as it's there when he needs it.

See if you and your spouse can relate to a few more of our differences.

TREY: I am an on-time person. By on time, I mean I want to be there 15 minutes before it starts.

LEA: If running late was an exercise, I'd be extremely fit.

TREY: I am a bit on the unorganized side.

LEA: I love organization. I think there is a place for everything, and everything should be in its place.

TREY: I don't need a lot of details to function in this world. I'm comfortable flying by the seat of my pants.

LEA: I love details. I want to know who, what, when, where, why, and how.

TREY: I am an extrovert, and I love getting up and speaking in front of crowds.

LEA: I am an introvert, and I still haven't figured out how Trey convinces me to get up and speak in front of crowds.

TREY: I am a morning person. Mornings make me happy. I love it when I actually wake up before my alarm goes off.

LEA: I'm a night owl. In fact, it's usually mid-morning before I decide if I'm even going to be a Christian for the day.☺

TREY: I fall asleep as soon as my head hits the pillow every night.

LEA: I'm extremely jealous of Trey's super power to fall asleep as soon as his head hits the pillow because it takes me forever to fall asleep.

TREY: I enjoy drinking coffee in the mornings.

LEA: I drink coffee in the mornings for the protection of other people.

TREY: I like to eat my cereal from a really big bowl, with a really big spoon.

LEA: I like to eat my cereal from a normal sized bowl, with a normal sized spoon, like a normal person. □

TREY: I'm a bit messy.

LEA: I'm a neat freak.

TREY: I like my coffee black.

LEA: I like my coffee with cream.

TREY: Tea must always be sweet.

LEA: I like my tea unsweetened.

TREY: I love to run.

LEA: The only time I'll be running is if I'm in fear for my life.

TREY: When I shop, I grab and go. (It's very dangerous for Lea to send me to the grocery store!)

LEA: When I shop, I like to read labels, compare prices, use coupons, and of course, when it comes to clothes, I try everything on (which drives Trey crazy).

During the first few years of marriage, our differences drove each other crazy! We spent the first few years of our marriage trying to fix one another and make the other person more like us. We saw our differences as weaknesses, instead of strengths. Despite our differences, we have learned that real intimacy in marriage truly happens when couples learn to accept and appreciate the differences in their spouse, instead of trying to "fix" them. When we began to truly understand and appreciate each other's personalities, we realized that my weaknesses were Trey's strengths, and vice versa.

For example, I am a very detailed person and good with numbers, so I manage our finances. Trey is completely fine with that because just the thought of reconciling a bank statement makes him antsy. On the other hand, Trey is a people person. He's very comfortable carrying on conversations and is a natural at complimenting people, so he gets to handle all of the phone calls regarding insurance, bills, satellite and internet services, etc. He can often get us discounts just by being nice and friendly. I get easily frustrated and would have us owing more money, if I had to make those kinds of phone calls. Since we have learned what each of us are good at, we try hard in our marriage to play to each other's strengths.

One of the best things a couple can do to strengthen their marriage, despite their differences, is to serve one another. When you learn to serve your spouse just the way your spouse likes to be served, you grow together as a couple. Did you catch that part "the way your spouse likes?"

Because of personality differences, every person likes to give and receive love in specific ways. Dr. Gary Chapman calls these "love languages." If you have not read the book The 5 Love Languages: The Secrets to Love that Lasts, it needs to be on your must-read list. The premise of the book is to speak your spouse's love language because every person has a primary love language they speak. Dr. Gary Chapman lists the five love languages as...

- **Physical Touch**
- **Quality Time**
- **Acts of Service**
- **Words of Affirmation**
- **Receiving Gifts**[1]

Every person needs all of these things, but most of the time we have a dominant love language that we speak. Trey's love language is physical touch, followed closely by words of affirmation. Lea's love language is acts of service, followed by quality time. Of course, we are different even in our love languages.

Speaking my love language may be as simple as patting me on the back, touching my shoulder, sitting close to me on the couch, etc. I love when my wife touches me.

Not long ago we were in charge of serving a meal to a large group of people. There were several working in the kitchen to prepare plates. I was on the plate detail team, adding a scoop of green beans to everyone's plate. The kitchen was full of chaos and people moving everywhere. Lea was in the kitchen with me but working in a different area. I began to notice that every time she would walk past me, she would run her hand across my back or touch my arm. I remember thinking to myself how much she loved me simply by the fact that she would reach out and touch me as she walked by. She was speaking my love language.

Interestingly enough, when I brought it up to her later that day, she stated she did not even notice that she was doing it. I love that she has learned to speak my love language so well that she does it without even being intentional at it.

Lea's love language on the other hand is acts of service. She loves when I do little things to serve her. She has told me often, "I love when you serve me in small ways because it makes me feel like you are taking care of me."

Some of the small things I have learned to do over time are things like keeping her car maintained and filled up with gas. I keep an eye on the gas gauge, and when it gets low, I fill it up for her so she doesn't have to.

I have learned that there are two types of people in this world: bed makers and people who think, "Why should I make the bed? I'm just going to get back in it tonight." Lea is the bed maker, while I fall into the other group. In the thirty years we have been married, she almost always makes the bed. Because her love language is acts of service, on occasion I sneak into the bedroom, while she is having her morning coffee and trying to decide if she's going to be a Christian for the day, and I make the bed. YES, I also put all seventy-two little pillows on it where they go. (Okay, that might be a slight exaggeration.)

A quick but very important side-note: If you are a perfectionist, do yourself and everyone else a favor by not criticizing your spouse or kids when they do things that don't quite measure up to your standards. They're trying to love you and serve you, so appreciate them for it and thank them. If you feel the need to "fix" what they did, do it when they aren't looking. When Trey makes the bed, he doesn't arrange all "seventy-two" pillows just the way I would, but that's okay! When he loads the dishwasher, he already knows I'll probably move things around, but I still appreciate that he put things in there. Speaking as a perfectionist myself, I have had to learn the hard way to loosen up, and my entire household is happier for it.

So back to love languages ... our friend Kristin's love language is gift giving. Not only does she give the most thoughtful gifts - because it's her love language - but her husband has had to learn the art of being a good gift giver. It is not about the amount of money you spend that matters; it's the thought behind the gift. When her husband goes to the store and doesn't just bring her a candy bar for a surprise, but brings her absolute favorite candy bar, that makes her day. The fact that her husband knows what she likes makes all the difference. If he stops off at Sonic and buys her a Route 44 Diet Coke with vanilla, cream and extra ice, and then shows up at her work to surprise her with it, he has nailed it. Her husband doing this for no reason what-so-ever, and knowing exactly how she likes her Sonic drink, is what makes this a very thoughtful gift to Kristin.

If your spouse's love language is words of

affirmation, then they need you to give them lots of praise. Tell them every day how awesome they are. Praise them all the time and for every little thing.

We had friends who struggled with this concept. His wife's love language is words of affirmation. I would try hard to explain to him how he needs to tell her every day that she is a good mom, beautiful, a great cook, etc. His response was always something along the lines of, "She is all those things, and she already knows it without me having to tell her." Giving praise didn't come easy to him, and it was difficult for him to grasp the concept of loving her the way she needed to be loved.

When it comes to meeting the needs of your spouse, you don't always have to understand why they need something in order to happily meet that need. You might not be good at speaking your spouse's love language because it's not your love language. Just because you aren't good at it, doesn't let you off the hook. Your spouse needs to be loved in their own special way, and you will have to be very intentional at meeting that need.

Kristin's husband will admit that he struggled with gift giving when they first married, but over time he has improved. Lea is not naturally a touchy, feely person, but as I mentioned earlier, speaking my love language of touch over the last thirty years has become second nature to her. The more you do it, the easier it will get. Practice really does make perfect!

If your spouse's love language is quality time, you must make time to spend with your spouse. Quality time means you are present with them when you are together, not just in the same room with them while you are looking at your phone. Your spouse will want to just hang out with you and do things together like good friends do as often as they can. Whatever your spouse's love language is, step up and speak it.

INSTANT MARRIAGE BOOST:

If you don't know your love language, you can take the quiz online for free at 5lovelanguages.com, but make sure you read the book as well.[2]

Serving one another is one of the healthiest things you can do for your marriage. Just today, Lea has brought me coffee, told me that I was awesome, squeezed my arm, and fixed me supper. I know she loves me because her actions show it. Just today, I was extra quiet this morning so she could sleep in. I reminded her that she is beautiful and filled her car up with gas. I love her, and she can tell by my actions. Marriage is about the little things. It will be as good as two people are willing to make it. Marriage is not always what you may think or hear in this world ... often it's even better.

If you have not seen the 5 love languages "taco" style or "coffee" style, we have included one here just for fun. (These have been shared all over social media so much that we are unable to credit the original source.)

Words of Affirmation: Your tacos are delicious.

Acts of Service: I made you tacos.

Receiving Gifts: Here's a taco.

Quality Time: Let's go out for tacos together.

Physical Touch: Let me hold you like a taco.

What to Do If You're Not Sure How to Serve Your Spouse

Sometimes we, especially husbands, struggle with how to best serve and love our spouse. As we mentioned in an earlier chapter, I struggled with this early in marriage. I thought the way to Lea's heart was through a big, expensive bouquet of flowers. It took a while for me to learn that she was content with a single rose. For her it was less about the gift or the money spent and more about serving her. What I finally learned to do was ask what I could do for her. Becoming a student of your spouse is one of the best things you can do for your marriage. Lea recalls one of the first times I did this ...

In the early days of our marriage, I remember Trey coming home one day from work. He walked in the front door, stepped over a pile of toys, walked past a sink full of dishes, and found me in the bedroom where I was folding a pile of laundry. After greeting me and visiting for a few moments, he asked, "Is there anything I can do around here to help you?"

I will be completely honest with you, that set me off a little. I was frustrated that he had not seen the toys, the dirty dishes, or the pile of laundry on the bed. What I had failed to appreciate was his willingness to help. When I finally realized that he honestly does not usually notice those types of things, and that he actually did want to help, I learned to just give him a job. I also realized when I praised him for a job well done, he was very likely to ask for another job. Remember from the previous chapter, men are motivated by your praise. He wanted to serve me; he was just unsure how.

(Side-note) Husbands, be extra helpful and patient when the house seems to be a wreck if you have little ones at home. Trey and I decided together that we would live on a tight budget, so I could stay home with our children and not work outside the home. I know there were days he would come home from work and wonder what in the world I had done all day because the house would be a small disaster. At times, I would spend an entire day coloring pictures, building Legos, playing dress-up, and reading stories with our kids. Please understand that those things are so much more important than doing laundry, dusting, and loading the dishwasher. Your wife probably needs you to help out around the house more than ever during this stage of life. Your kids are only little for a season, and that season will pass all too quickly.

Treat Your Spouse Better Than They Deserve Because That's How God Treats You Every Day

There will be days when you don't feel it, and that's okay because love is an action, not a feeling. On those days when you don't feel it, choose to love anyway. On those days when your differences are driving you crazy, choose to love anyway. On those days when your spouse seems unlovable, choose to love anyway.

Enjoy serving your spouse and do it with a joyful attitude. Let's say you approach your spouse and say, "Honey, I need such and such from you," and then they roll their eyes, scrunch up their nose, question you, make a snide remark, or just ignore you. When any of these things happen, the spouse with a need feels rejected. No one wants their needs met by their spouse when their spouse sees it as a chore, duty or obligation. Meet your spouse's needs with a good attitude.

The thirteenth chapter of the book of John has always been an amazing story to us. It is the story of Jesus washing his disciples' feet. Washing feet would have been the job of a servant or a slave. Someone had prepared the banquet supper but forgot to get a servant to wash feet. Can't you see Peter coming in and thinking to himself, "Don't ask

me to wash feet. I am Peter, one of the three."
Maybe James and John came in and thought, "We
are the sons of thunder. You can't expect us to
wash feet." No one stepped up to wash feet that
night ... no one except Jesus.

*"So he got up from the meal, took off his outer
clothing, and wrapped a towel around his waist.
After that, he poured water into a basin and began
to wash his disciples' feet, drying them with the
towel that was wrapped around him."* (John 13:4-
5, NIV)

That must have made the disciples extremely
uncomfortable. The one who was their Lord had
become their servant. Peter did not like it at all and
told Jesus, "You shall never wash my feet." Jesus
did wash his feet and the feet of all the other
disciples there as well.

We are bringing up this story because there is a
really good lesson here which a lot of people
miss. The lesson is that Jesus chose to wash the
feet of Judas as well. He did not come to Judas
and say, "I know you are going to betray me, and
there is no way I am washing your feet." Yes, he
knew Judas was going to betray him, and he
washed his feet anyway. Jesus treated his
betrayer better than he deserved, and he does the
exact same with us every day.

Nearly every day I pick up something Trey has left down ... clothes on the floor that he could have put in the hamper, a hairbrush that was left out instead of being put back in the drawer, and shoes wherever he kicked them off the night before. There were times, as a young wife and mother, that this was a great source of irritation and contention.

Then something happened that totally changed my perspective. Within the same month, two of my high school friends lost their husbands, one very unexpectedly and the other after a battle with cancer. These friends of mine would give anything to pick up their husbands' shoes or dirty clothes from the floor again! They would give anything to see their husbands, hug them, or just hear their voices again. Now when I find myself getting a little irritated because I'm having to pick up or clean up after my husband, I remind myself just how blessed I am to have a husband I can serve today.

Another perspective on serving your spouse is that you are really serving Jesus when you pick up the shoes or clean up the mess. *"Work willingly at whatever you do, as though you were working for the Lord rather than for people. Remember that the Lord will give you an inheritance as your reward, and that the Master you are serving is*

Christ." (Colossians 3:23-24, NLT) This was addressed to slaves during that time, but in light of all Jesus has done for us, I think it can apply to marriage as well.

Should your spouse pick up after himself or herself? Yes, they probably should, but sometimes we do the right thing simply because it's the right thing to do, and we don't wait for our spouse to make the first move. Romans 5:8 tells us that "While we were still sinners, Christ died for us." (NIV) He didn't wait for us to get our act together. He made the first move because he loves us. Pam Farrell puts this so well, "When a relationship is based only on behaviors, *no one* can stay good long enough to succeed. Love's grace trumps human imperfection."[3] Treat your spouse better than they deserve because that's how Jesus treats you every day.

Make sure that when you are serving your spouse, you are not keeping score. God doesn't keep score. God never looks down and says, "I have blessed you ten times today, and you've only blessed me three times." Aren't we glad God doesn't keep score this way? We cannot keep up with God's goodness. We will never be able to out give God, so make sure you aren't keeping score with your spouse. We don't think God ever intended for marriage to be a "you scratch my back, and I'll scratch yours" relationship.

For years people have said marriage is fifty/fifty ... give fifty percent and take fifty percent. That is a horrible concept. Maybe that is why the divorce rate has been so high. If anything, marriage should be about giving one hundred percent of everything you have. Marriage as God intended is treating your spouse better than they deserve because that's how God treats you. Love and serve your spouse as Christ loved you.

A new command I give you: Love one another. As I have loved you, so you must love one another.

(John 13:34, NIV)

...serve one another humbly in love.

(Galatians 5:13, NIV)

8 – KEEP FIRST THINGS FIRST

Don't backburner your marriage! It is so easy in this day and time to get our priorities totally out-of-whack. We are busy people in busy families, and we go one hundred miles per hour from morning until night. Sometimes we allow life to get in the way of marriage. What is life? Life is:

* Work

* Hobbies

* Children

* Summer Activities

* Paying Bills

* Little League

* School

* Church functions, etc.

*Volunteer Work

None of these are bad things, unless we allow them to take priority over our marriage. You may own your home and cars. You may have a big retirement fund and a good job, but your greatest treasures on this earth are your relationships ... your spouse, your kids, your family.

You Are Rich in Relationships

Several years ago, I met a man that was a multi-millionaire. I think he was the first millionaire I'd ever met. I'll admit I was a bit in awe of him when I found out how much money he had. He told me about his plane, multiple houses, and other things which impressed me. As we visited, I learned he was in his early fifties, had never married, and that his greatest desire was to marry and have a family. He'd even been on the television show Millionaire Matchmaker hoping to find just the perfect woman. He told me he had lots of women to choose from, but none of them had really "clicked" with him, so I tried to encourage him, "Be patient; it'll happen."

I'll be honest, my only thoughts throughout our conversation were, "This guy is living the dream," and "He's got it all ... he's a multi-millionaire with houses in Miami and Los Angeles. He has a plane that flies him anywhere he wants to go. He's been on television and has his pick of women. He has everything that money can buy."

At the end of our conversation, my wife and four sons came up, and he asked about them. "Is this your family? All these boys are yours?" I was a bit taken aback by his question, so I tried to explain. I told him I had married my high school sweetheart; we had four amazing sons, and that we were still madly in love today. Right then he looked me in the eyes and said something I'll never forget. His words literally rocked my world and made me rethink everything that I thought was important. He simply said, "I hope you understand, you are richer than I will ever be."

He was absolutely right. I have what money can't buy. I am rich in marriage, rich in family, and was by far the richest person there that day. May we never forget that our relationships are the most valuable things we have. I'm reminded of Proverbs 18:22, *"A man's greatest treasure is his wife--she is a gift from the Lord."* (CEV)

We visit with people all the time who didn't realize

their marriage was the most valuable thing they had until it was threatened or lost. Value your marriage and protect it by all means possible. It is the most valuable thing you have on this earth. Valuing your marriage means more than just staying faithful; it also means seeing your marriage as a priority. It means being willing to work on it and willing to help it grow.

Make Your Marriage A Priority Over Your Children

We will never forget our visit with a young couple who was needing help. They had come seeking advice for their marriage. They were struggling big time and needing direction and guidance. Their marriage was "hanging on by a thread" ... their words, not ours.

They were going to spend the upcoming Saturday with us at a marriage workshop we were doing. We told them this would be a great jumpstart for their marriage to help get it back on the right track. They totally agreed. We prayed for them all week, excited that they would be going with us. We love seeing couples who are willing to work on their marriages, struggling or not.

The day before the workshop we got the dreaded

call. They were not going to go to the workshop after all. Someone had scheduled a last-minute make-up baseball game for their son's Little League team. "We just hate to miss a game," they said. "We go to every game possible, so he will know that we love and support him." We tried to convince them that coming to a workshop that could help their struggling marriage was more important than one single game. We even asked the question, "There will be other games, right?" They said there would be, but they didn't want to miss any of them. Despite all our begging and pleading for them to come with us, they chose to go watch their child play baseball.

Fast forward nine months later, when I received a text from them saying they had filed for divorce. We can't say that going to our marriage workshop on a Saturday would have fixed all the problems, but it would've been a good start. Instead, they chose to put their marriage on the back burner in order to put their child first. We couldn't help but wonder what their child would've thought. Would he have chosen to have his parents attend his game or work on their marriage? We think he would want his mother and father to still be married and for them to be a family more than anything else.

We see this all the time in our ministry. People

who push their marriage to the back burner of the stove in order to give their children one hundred percent of their attention and focus solely on their kids. The rule is pretty simple: if you put your marriage first, your marriage and your kids will benefit. If you put your kids first, your marriage and your kids may suffer in the long run.

Some might call us traditional in our beliefs. We believe God comes first, our marriage second, and children third. While many people see this as the correct order, there are some that struggle with putting their children after their marriage, especially those who have already been in a failed marriage. They feel as if their children are the only ones in this world who haven't let them down or betrayed them, and they can't imagine putting anyone before their kids. Many believe children should come before marriage no matter what. This is a dangerous concept that we will cover in this chapter.

When we encourage you to put your marriage before your kids, we don't mean you should neglect your children. There is absolutely no greater ministry in this world than raising kids! It is a wonderful and amazing responsibility. We have raised four sons, and it's a huge blessing to watch them fly and do life on their own. Our job as parents is to work ourselves out of a job, but our job as parents is also to teach our children about marriage by example. Our children cannot just see us as a mom and dad only. They also need to see us as husband and wife. Children need to see their parents dating, being affectionate, praying with one another, kissing, laughing, going away for a weekend together, etc.

Your children are enrolled in "How to Do Marriage" school, and you are their teacher, so work hard to show them what a healthy marriage looks like. Did you know your children are watching you?

- They are watching how you do marriage.
- They notice the tone of voice you use with your spouse.
- They are watching if you're affectionate with your spouse.
- They are watching how you talk about and treat your spouse.

The story about the couple who chose to go to their son's game instead of a marriage workshop is an example of how often times parents put children in front of their marriage. Many parents will tell you, "We want to give one hundred percent of our attention to our kids because we only have them for a short period of time." We don't disagree with this. You do only have them for a short while, but you have to make your marriage a priority during those years, so that you still have a strong marriage when the nest is empty.

There seems to be a spike in the divorce rate for couples who are experiencing empty nest. Some couples base their entire marriage around their children and their children's activities, and they drift apart in the process. They know they have drifted apart, but many stay together for the sake of the kids. Once the last child leaves home, they divorce. They had zero relationship with one another outside of their children. Empty nest came and with it an empty marriage.

Meet Mike and Sarah. They were good parents. They wanted the best for their kids. They put their kids first in their life and repeatedly said to one another, "Someday when the kids are gone, we'll focus on our marriage. We will go on dates, take trips, and do fun things together, but right now we must give all of the time and energy we have to the kids."

Their world revolved around work and their kids. There was no time for dating as husband and wife because they had kids to take here and there. Their kids were involved in every activity that was available. Mike and Sarah literally dropped into bed every night exhausted from their fast-paced lifestyle and trying to meet all the needs of their children. There wasn't much intimacy in their marriage as husband and wife. They were just too tired and busy for that. They did life together, paid bills together, and raised kids together, but there was no real spark between them anymore. Mike and Sarah had become roommates and not soulmates. They had made the mistake of moving their marriage to the back burner with good intentions of focusing on their marriage when their kids were gone.

Fast forward several years ...

One year after their last child left for college, Mike and Sarah split up ... twenty-five years of marriage gone. They said there was no longer any spark. The problem was that they had not maintained their relationship together outside of raising children. They had no common interests any more. They had always thought, "When the kids are gone and we're empty-nesters, we'll get back to marriage and focus on one another. That's when we'll have time to do some things together." What they hadn't realized was when empty nest hit, they had an empty marriage, simply from not giving their marriage any attention.

Make sure you don't miss the point. We are not saying kids are a hassle or children are a burden. We are saying, don't make the mistake of waiting until your children are grown and gone to focus on your marriage. Don't get so caught up in raising kids that you don't do marriage. Date, spend time together, develop common interests, get away for an occasional weekend, flirt, touch, be intimate. As we said earlier, it's not only healthy for your marriage, it's also healthy for your kids to see you nurturing your marriage.

We were fascinated watching a couple one night at Red Lobster. They had to be in their seventies and couldn't keep their hands off one another. They held hands, touched, shared bites of food and looked into one another's eyes. As they walked by our table to leave, Trey told them, "I just have to say I loved watching you two. You are obviously still so in love." They both blushed, and said thank you for noticing. This was their date night. I couldn't help but think, "What a great feeling to take each other by the hand when you're in your seventies and say, "WE MADE IT."

Don't be satisfied just being part of the fifty percent who stay married. Work hard to be in the percentage who are happily married.

Be A Good Forgiver

They say there are three rules to being successful

in real estate: location, location, and location. There are also three rules to being successful in marriage: forgiveness, forgiveness, and forgiveness. You probably know this, but you did not marry a perfect person. Before you say amen, also realize your spouse did not marry a perfect person either. That makes forgiveness an essential part of marriage. To be a good forgiver you must learn to ...

- Forgive when your spouse apologizes.

- Forgive before they have a chance to apologize.

- Forgive even if they don't apologize.

Jesus was this type of forgiver, and believe it or not, He asks us to be the same. In all four Gospels, Jesus tells us that we have to forgive others if we want God's forgiveness. Matthew includes the story of the Unmerciful Servant in which a man, who had just been forgiven an enormous debt by the king, did not forgive the debt of another man and had him thrown into jail. When the king found out what the forgiven man had done, he had him thrown into jail to be tortured until his debt could be paid. Jesus concludes this story with a less than comforting moral, *"So my heavenly Father will also do to every one of you, if you do not forgive your brother or sister from your heart."* (Matthew 18:35, NIV)

Jesus also said on the cross as He was dying, *"Father, forgive them; for they do not know what they are doing."* (Luke 23:34, NIV) Forgiveness is a characteristic of a Jesus follower, and it is an *essential* part of marriage.

Several years ago, on a Sunday morning as we were getting ready for church, I went into a small closet where my sports jackets hung. Before I had a chance to shut the door, Lea said with a sharp tone, "Please shut the door all the way. You always leave it cracked." First, I didn't realize I hadn't been shutting it all the way. Second, the tone I thought she used was a little harsh. I was aggravated, so I actually shut the door with a little extra push. I didn't slam it, but I came close as I gritted my teeth choosing not to say anything.

The following Sunday I was back in that closet again. As soon as I opened the door, my frustrations from the previous week came back. I replayed the whole scenario in my head again. I found myself again shutting the door with a little extra force, so she could *hear* that I had not left it cracked. This went on for the next three Sundays. Every Sunday I felt angry when I opened the closet door. I realized that my unwillingness to forgive was causing hurt in our relationship. Had she asked me for forgiveness? No, but did I need to forgive? Yes.

I remember calling her into the room and apologizing to her for being angry with her. I told her the whole story that had happened the previous month, and that every time I had used that closet, I had gotten angry with her again. I told her I was very sorry. Now get this, when I told her about the whole closet ordeal, she did not remember one drop of it ... not the conversation, not the tone, nothing.

We often walk around with anger and bitterness over something that our spouse or someone else has done, and they don't even know they've really done anything. We are hurting ourselves more than we are hurting them by being bitter. As the old saying goes, being bitter and choosing not to forgive, is like drinking poison and expecting it to hurt the other person.

Marriages often fail when couples constantly focus on what their spouse does wrong instead of what their spouse does right ... and fail in the area of forgiveness.

Maybe you've been hurt by your spouse, and it's more than something trivial like a harsh tone for leaving a closet door open. Maybe you're in a marriage where there has been dishonesty, lies or unfaithfulness. We totally understand those issues are not just something that is easy to get over. It takes years to both get past the hurt and rebuild the trust. If you have chosen to stick with your marriage and fight through issues like this, we admire and applaud you. We are inspired by you! Not every marriage has to end just because there is a reason. Learn to work through your bitterness and anger, seek counseling, and be patient with your healing process. It's so very important for your sake not to revel in your bitterness and anger. Work to move past it. Work to no longer hold it against them. Will that be easy? No, but it can be done.

We know several couples that have been through infidelity, but chose to work through it in order to save their marriages. Unfaithfulness wreaks havoc on a relationship and is one of the hardest things to forgive, but these couples worked hard through these struggles, and in time were able to forgive. Here is a quote from a dear friend who was determined to save her marriage:

"Fight for your marriage.

Figure out how to do unconditional love.

Hang in there through the hard times,

so you can enjoy the good times.

Find out what a Godly marriage looks like

and mimic it. Marriage isn't easy, but it's worth it.

Don't settle...work hard at it, so you can have

the kind of marriage your heart so desires!"

~Ashley

She wrote that on Facebook, as well as proudly posted pictures of her and her husband together on their fourteenth wedding anniversary about two years after learning her husband had been unfaithful. We are grateful they gave us permission to tell their story in hopes of inspiring others to fight for their marriage even during the toughest of times. They understand the importance of forgiveness and the true value of marriage done well.

INSTANT MARRIAGE BOOST:

Are you harboring some kind of grudge against your spouse? Whether it's big or small, pray right now and ask God to help you forgive.

Husbands, Protect Your Marriage

Husbands: The most precious possession that

ever comes to a man in this world is a woman's heart. Protect it, guard it, and never take it for granted. Wear your wedding ring, if your job allows it. If it's a safety hazard at work, then wear it when you're not working. Let the world know you are honored to be married to your wife. Wear your wedding ring and your marriage like a badge of honor. Loving and serving your wife and family does not mean you are "whipped." It's called being a husband. It's very sexy and very manly!

My wedding ring is a simple gold band that I never take off. If you look at my ring closely, you'll notice that it looks a bit rough. You won't see any diamonds or engravings, but what you will see are nicks, scrapes and dings. Those nicks, scrapes and dings symbolize the joy and pain from our years of marriage. They represent struggles, hopes, dreams, and promises. My ring looks good when it's cleaned and polished, but I'm more comfortable with it looking like the 30 plus years of marriage that we've built.

The simple band of gold, placed on my hand by my wife on our wedding day, represents so much more than a ceremony of marriage; it symbolizes the family we've built. My ring reminds me I can hold her hand or touch her any time because she is mine. It reminds me that we're a team, and that we work better together than apart. It reminds me that I'm totally committed to her, and she's committed to me. The ring reminds me that throughout the past 30 years, whether it's the highs of the births of our sons or the lows of dealing with cancer, we have been there for one another through both better and worse.

- The value of my old ten-carat gold men's wedding band, purchased back in 1988 when we had no money, is probably about one hundred dollars.
- The price paid to have it polished once every few years is about twenty dollars.
- Constantly having it on my hand to remind me that I'm the luckiest man in the world ... PRICELESS.

A man's greatest treasure is his wife—she is a gift from the Lord.

(Proverbs 18:22, CEV)

9 – FRIENDSHIP MATTERS

Have you ever given much thought to some of the ridiculous myths in this world that we seem to tell to children? Myths like ...

- If you swallow your gum, it won't come out for seven years. (Who even makes up stuff like that? We have changed enough diapers to know where you can find gum a couple of days or so after a little one swallows it.)

- If you make an ugly face, it might freeze.

- If you cross your eyes, they might stick.

- If you play with matches, you will wet the bed. (Before I married Trey, I had never heard this in my life! Trey likes to joke that most of his childhood was ruined by this myth. He never played with matches for fear of wetting the bed. He jokingly says there were times he woke up as a child and thought, "Hey! I don't remember playing with matches yesterday!")

Apparently great-great grandmothers centuries ago all across the globe made up all such myths in order to control the behavior of their little children.

There are some crazy myths when it comes to marriage as well. Here are a few terrible ones that some people tend to believe:

- If you just ignore or deny that you're having problems, they will eventually go away.

- Great marriages just happen, they don't take work.

- The grass is greener on the other side.

- Now that I'm married, I don't have to work as hard at the relationship.

- And the big one that we want to talk about ... you shouldn't marry your best friend.

Never underestimate the importance that friendship plays in your marriage because the very best marriages are built on friendship. Before Trey and I married, we dated for four years. We were high school sweethearts, but we were also friends. We went to church together, took family vacations together, and just loved spending time together. As our relationship matured, so did our friendship. We went from being good friends to best friends. Our friendship has been one of the main foundations for our marriage over the last 30 plus years.

The world is learning, and studies are showing, that a marriage built on friendship is a happier marriage. A 2014 study by The National Bureau of Economic Research showed, "Married individuals who consider their spouse to be their best friend have higher life satisfaction scores."[1]

Building a friendship for us has not always been easy. We have had to work hard to build and find similar interests. As mentioned in an earlier chapter, we are very different people with different likes and interests. There has been a lot of compromise from both of us to learn to have similar interests, but over time our friendship has deepened.

It's Hard to Have A Good Marriage Unless You Actually Spend Time with the Person You're Married To

Friendship is built by spending time together. Another terrible marriage myth we didn't previously mention is "absence makes the heart grow fonder." Absence is actually hard on marriage. We're not talking about being apart for a few hours here and there. We are talking about long absences. Some people have jobs or military service that require them to be gone for long periods of time, and they have to work extra hard to keep their marriage friendship strong.

Trey had a man sit in his office years ago and tell him that he was moving because he had accepted an offer for a better paying job. Trey congratulated him and told him that we were going to sure miss him and his family. The man replied, "Oh, my family is not coming with me. My wife has a good job here, and my kids can't bear the thought of going to new schools." He continued, "I'll be able to come home for a whole week out of each month to see them."

Trey encouraged him to think this over long and hard. He told him that being absent from his family for long periods of time would be hard on his marriage and little girls. He replied, "We have a good marriage, and did I mention that this will double my salary?" Exactly one year later, that same man sat back in Trey's office. He was there to find help for his marriage that was crumbling. He wanted nothing more than to save his family.

Of course, not every story like this has a sad ending. There are couples who are able to make long absences work, but our point is this: if at all possible, avoid long absences from each other because they are hard on your family.

Nineteenth century German philosopher, Friedrich Nietzsche, said, "It is not a lack of love, but a lack of friendship that makes unhappy marriages." It's really hard to have a good marriage unless you actually spend time with the person you're married to. What are some things you and your spouse like to do together? What are your spouse's hobbies? What does he or she love to do? Does your spouse have a regular workout routine? Does he or she walk or jog?

We recommend you try joining your spouse in whatever activity it is they love doing. Putting out great effort, even if you can't keep up at first, will draw your spouse toward you because it shows you care. You are likely to find some satisfaction in taking part in your spouse's most enjoyable moments and activities.

We met a lady at one of our seminars in Arkansas who mentioned to us that she and her husband really never did anything together. That bothered her, as it should have. She mentioned that she would love for him to go to a concert with her but all he ever wanted to do was go deer hunting. We asked her, "Why have you not gone deer hunting with him?" She explained that he used to ask all the time, but he'd finally given up on her because she always told him that was the last thing she wanted to do. We encouraged her to give deer hunting a try, and after she went with him she could ask him to go to a concert with her. We told her there was no guarantee he would say yes, but it was worth a try. We also said, "You are not allowed to complain or gripe while on the trip. You go and pretend to have fun even if you don't."

We got an email from her about a month later. She had gone on her first deer hunt. Her exact words were, "Surprisingly, I actually enjoyed it." She mentioned getting to watch the sun come up with her husband, drink coffee in a deer stand, and watch the wildlife awaken. She said most of all she enjoyed getting to spend the whole morning with her husband, and he had enjoyed it as well. She concluded her email saying, "He has agreed to go with me to a concert this Thursday." We encourage you to try something you don't think you will like; you may be surprised that you actually like it after all.

If It's Important to Your Spouse, It Should Be Important to You

Whether it is a hobby, a project at work, sports, or a TV series ... if your spouse is interested in it, you should have some interest in it as well.

A few years back when Pinterest came out, it was like a new toy that I could not put down, but Trey was totally lost on what Pinterest was. He referred to Pinterest as crack cocaine for women because my friends and I seemed to be fascinated with it. Since I talked about Pinterest so much, Trey signed up so he could get a better understanding of it. He may very well have been the first man to sign up for Pinterest. His buddies gave him a hard time and teased that they were taking his man card from him, but I love the fact that my husband was willing to learn about something new that I was interested in.

Trey has learned to watch HGTV with me, go to huge flea markets, repurpose old furniture, and do other things that weren't at the top of his list. Why would he do this? Because best friends like to spend time together. "Happy is the man who finds a best friend, and far happier is he who finds that best friend in his wife." ~ Franz Schubert

About fifteen years ago when football season ended and before baseball season had started, Trey began watching NASCAR. Some of his friends were big fans and had him watching on Sundays. I'll be honest ... at the time, I would have rather watched the toilet brush go around in circles in the toilet than I would have to watch those cars go around in circles on those race tracks.

When I realized the Sunday afternoon activity of NASCAR watching was not going away, I sat down and began to watch. I tried to learn the drivers and the rules, etc. Before too long I thought, "This isn't too bad." Trey and I traveled to watch a race only a few hours from where we lived, and we had a blast. The sights, sounds, and smell of burning rubber were even more fun in person. Over the next few years, I suggested taking other trips to various places to watch some races. We enjoyed trips to Bristol, Vegas, Richmond, and other places doing something we had learned to love together. Simply by be willing to try something my husband enjoyed, we got some amazing trips out of the deal, but most of all, we got to build a deeper friendship by spending time together.

If conversation with your spouse is at the top of your list of emotional needs, as it is for many women, then building mutual interests is even more essential. One of the biggest perks of having common interests and doing things together is the conversation that it provides. If I had never tried to take an interest in sports, I would miss out on so many conversations with my husband and sons! Not only have I taken an interest, but we watch games together on TV, attend games together when we are able, and even play fantasy sports together online. The more interests you have in common, the more things you will have to talk about.

Do not underestimate the importance of being friends with your spouse. Have fun together! Don't just work together and chase kids together; do fun things together too. Finding things to do together where you can build your friendship even stronger is essential. Whether you're singing at the top of your lungs at a concert, taking a walk in the park, or simply having coffee together, make time to have fun with your best friend.

INSTANT MARRIAGE BOOST:

If you need help discovering some common interests or just want to try it for fun, search for the Recreational Enjoyment Inventory at MarriageBuilders.com and work through the quick survey.[2] There are 122 activities listed with space to add others. You and your spouse rate your interest level in each activity. The activities that receive a high rating from both of you are things you should pursue. You might be surprised to discover you are interested in something that you never realized your spouse is also interested in!

Six Ways to Be Your Spouse's Best Friend

How can you work more towards being your spouse's best friend? Here are some suggestions that build a solid foundation of friendship in marriage:

1. DATE. We talked a lot about dating in a previous chapter, but it is a big deal. Date and have some fun together, but guard against your date night looking like this ...

Wife: What do you want to do tonight?

Husband: Whatever is fine with me.

Wife: I don't care. It's up to you.

Husband: It makes me no difference. You decide.

Wife: Well, what is something that we could do?

Husband: Anything is fine. Just pick something already!

Wife: If you're going to act like that, I don't want to go.

Husband: Fine.

Take turns planning your date nights, or maybe one of you picks the restaurant and the other picks the activity. (Refer back to "12 Great Date Night Ideas" in Chapter 2 for some other dating ideas.) Dating provides time for conversation, affection, and fun. Don't miss out on this opportunity to grow your friendship.

2. GET EXCITED ABOUT THE THINGS YOUR SPOUSE GETS EXCITED ABOUT. Even if it isn't your thing, give it a try. If your husband loves baseball, take an interest in baseball. If your wife likes gardening, take an interest in gardening. You may find out you like these things after all.

3. KNOW YOUR SPOUSE'S WEAKNESSES AND LOVE THEM ANYWAY.

Isn't that what best friends are for? *"A friend loves at all times..."* (Proverbs 17:17, NIV) We all need someone in our corner who knows the best and the worst about us, and will be there for us no matter what.

4. GIVE YOUR SPOUSE PRAISE.

Compliment them! Build them up! Aren't you naturally drawn to people who make you feel good about yourself? Be that person to your spouse. Affirm your spouse's best qualities, and celebrate their wins. That's what best friends do for each other.

5. OFFER FORGIVENESS AND GRACE.

Everyone has a bad day, says hurtful things, or disappoints us on occasion. Offer the grace and forgiveness to your spouse in those moments that you would want in return.

6. PUT YOUR SPOUSE FIRST.

Isn't that the whole concept of a *best* friend? Your best friend is at the top of your list, your #1, your first choice of people you want to spend time with. Don't let your spouse become just one of your friends. Make them your best friend.

We met Mr. & Mrs. Ross in Tennessee a few

years ago. They were a sweet, older couple who were both in their early nineties. They'd been married over seventy years. They both still lived in their own home without any help, but the last three years had been tough on Mrs. Ross. During those past three years she had lost most of her eyesight. This made life harder on Mr. Ross because now he had to do all the cooking, a job she once did. She also had rheumatoid arthritis, so she struggled with being able to help around the house at all, and couldn't even dress herself.

Mr. and Mrs. Ross came to one of our Stronger Marriage Workshops. They sat down close to the front. In between class sessions, we had a chance to visit with them. We found out that he was now taking care of her every need one hundred percent of the time. He would pick out her clothes, help her get dressed, and still take care of all the other chores around the house.

Trey asked Mr. Ross, "Why have you come to our workshop today? You are already such an inspiring husband." His response was amazing. He simply said, "She has been my best friend for over 70 years, and I thought there might be something new I could learn today to help me serve her better."

We got a little teary eyed as we listened to Mr.

Ross talk about their special relationship. How could we not? Here was a man who was now doing both his and his wife's jobs at home. He was caring for her full time, and he showed up at a marriage workshop looking for a new way to serve his best friend.

Marriage isn't about having a fancy wedding, a nice home, or a white picket fence. Marriage is about friendship, hospital stays, fighting through the tough times, being there for one another, and staying through it all.

May God raise up more couples like Mr. and Mrs. Ross who teach us about love, service, and friendship.

There is no more lovely, friendly, and charming relationship, communion or company than a good marriage.

~Martin Luther King

10 – THE OVERLOOKED INTIMACY

Sex is often the first thing we think of when we hear the word "intimacy." Most people don't realize that there are many forms of intimacy which lead to an extraordinary marriage. One that's often overlooked is spiritual intimacy. Spiritual intimacy thrives when couples share faith together and observe religious practices. Spiritual intimacy is an amazing thing that many couples miss out on because they either don't understand it or realize how powerful it can be in their marriage.

When Lea and I think back on some of our most intimate moments over the past thirty years, they aren't always sexual. Many times, they have been spiritual. We cannot imagine being married without our faith and without God. Our marriage, just like every other marriage, has seen its ups and downs. Like you, we have struggled with some things that life has thrown at us. Like it or not, problems are a part of life, marriage, and family. The truth is, you WILL have problems, but you can choose joy instead of despair and still have a happy, healthy marriage even in the midst of those problems when you rely upon God and your faith.

Lea and I have personally dealt with...

- the passing of both our mothers after lengthy illnesses.

- the struggles of miscarriage.

- a son who unexpectedly decided to leave college and join the military - entering a dangerous career as a Special Operations Army Ranger. (While we are very proud of his choice, it wasn't something we understood at the time).

- cancer...twice.

- children who aren't perfect and have made mistakes.

- thirty years of differing opinions.

We could go on and on. Despite some struggles, problems, and trials, we chose to put our faith in God. We chose not to focus on the problems, but on the love that we have for one another. Problems will come and go, but love and faith will stick through thick and thin. Our goal for the past thirty years has been to build our family and marriage on a foundation of faith in God.

> *"Therefore everyone who hears these words of mine and puts them into practice is like a wise man who built his house on the rock. The rain came down, the streams rose, and the winds blew and beat against that house; yet it did not fall, because it had its foundation on the rock. But everyone who hears these words of mine and does not put them into practice is like a foolish man who built his house on sand. The rain came down, the streams rose, and the winds blew and beat against that house, and it fell with a great crash."* (Matthew 7:24-27, NIV)

We understand that storms come; we've seen them and felt them. Building the foundation of our home on faith has helped us stand through the storms. When the storms come, will your house stand? Storms often cause us to do one of these three things: deny our faith, doubt our faith, or depend on our faith. We highly recommend that you *depend* on your faith. Build your marriage and family on The Rock.

Spiritual Intimacy with Your Spouse Can Be A Struggle

I was not good at being spiritually intimate with Lea in the early years of our marriage. Neither of us talked about it much, but we knew we were lacking in spiritual intimacy. We prayed and read the Bible with other people, but Lea and I didn't do these things *together* as a couple. Our relationship with Jesus was a top priority, but we never seemed to freely share our faith with each other.

I will never forget the time that it all came to a head. My wife tearfully said, "We pray with other people, but why don't we ever pray with each other?" My heart was broken. I felt like a failure. I was failing to be the spiritual leader in my family. Things changed from that moment on. We had always worshiped together and attended church together, but we finally began to pray together and read the Bible together. Things turned around for us, but it took some tears from my wife to get my attention.

Maybe our situation sounds familiar. You have

faith ... maybe you both pray and read your Bibles separately, but you're not doing it together. We want to encourage you to strengthen your spiritual intimacy with one another.

This has become such an important issue to us that we make a very big deal out of it in our workshops. Part of our follow up five-day homework for couples who attend our workshop is that they pray together. We don't ask couples to sit down and have long prayer sessions together. That may come in time. Initially, however, we ask that they start with a simple prayer.

Some couples are not comfortable praying together because they have never done it. If this is the case for you and your spouse, then we encourage you to start by taking each other's hand when you go to bed at night and say a short prayer: "Dear God, thank you for my spouse and my family. Please bless us. In Jesus' name, Amen." How simple is that? You can do it with the lights out and keep it short and sweet. It's a good place to start, and once you start, you'll find that it gets easier and easier. Your prayers will become more comfortable and heartfelt. Your spiritual intimacy will grow as you build the habit of praying together.

We recently received a letter from a lady who

attended one of our workshops in Oklahoma. Here's what she had to say about praying with her husband: "Thanks for challenging us to pray with one another. We have loved starting our day off in prayer together and how much more peaceful our day goes because of it. Plus ... you can't get a much better feeling than knowing your husband has prayed specifically over you every day!"

Benefits of Praying Together

I absolutely love praying with my wife now. I hate that I missed out on it for several years early in our marriage. I not only love praying with my wife, I also adore listening to her pray. When we pray together, it allows us to see into the secret place of each other's heart that is usually reserved only for God.

Lea praying for me is a highlight of my life. Whenever I have to leave for a speaking engagement, or I have stress in my life, or I am struggling with something, Lea will say, "Let me pray for you about this."

She has prayed with me in good times and in tough times. In 2003, I spent a year battling cancer for the second time. The second time was much more difficult. I had an initial surgery, followed by a second very big surgery that required a week-long hospital stay. I spent a few days in ICU and practically an entire summer in my recliner trying to recover.

Despite having four young boys, Lea never left my side. Every day she would take time to pray for me. That summer, I learned that real love is not the stuff you see in the movies or on television. Rather, it was my wife telling me I looked great to her even though I was pale, skinny, sick, and too weak to do a thing. Real love was her willingness to pray for me every single day. I cannot imagine going through that summer without having a spiritual partner by my side.

Maybe it is time for you to step up in your marriage and be the spiritual partner that your spouse has wanted and needed. Talk to your spouse about this. Maybe you've brought up the subject before with no results. If so, try again. I challenge you today to be that person. I challenge you to take your marriage beyond just physical, and make it spiritual as well. Don't miss out on the power and intimacy that come from praying together.

Marriages and families today don't need a small dose of God; they need a large dose of God. It is hard to have a "marriage made in heaven," if you don't allow God to play a major role in it.

Pray Specifically

One of the things we talk about in our family workshop is praying specifically for different areas of your marriage and family. We would like to share a few specific things for which you can pray. You can pray about these together, or during your own personal quiet time. Since there are seven specific things, you may want to focus on one for each day of the week.

7 Things to Pray for Your Marriage & Family

1. Thank God for your marriage.

2. Ask God to bless your marriage and to help you be the best spouse you can be. (Remember you can only change yourself, not your spouse.)

3. Ask God to give you wisdom as a spouse and as a parent and in all the decisions you make.

4. Pray for your children by name, asking God to give them wisdom and to surround them with godly friends.

5. Pray for your future together as husband and wife because your relationship will continually change throughout different stages of life.

6. Pray that you will keep your priorities straight.

7. Ask God to protect your marriage from Satan because marriages are being destroyed every day.

Specifically praying for your marriage and family is one of the best things you can do. Never underestimate the power of prayer.

INSTANT MARRIAGE BOOST:

Take a moment right now to pray for your spouse.

Worship Together

Attending church together and worshiping together provides another important avenue to help you grow spiritually. Bible class lessons and sermons can provide great material for you and your spouse to discuss concerning God's word and your faith. This can help enhance your spiritual intimacy by providing wisdom and direction for your marriage and family.

Encourage One Another To Grow Spiritually

Any time you have the opportunity to go on a church retreat, a ladies' conference or a men's conference, go! Encourage your spouse to go. These kinds of things spur us on and rekindle a desire to be the best version of ourselves that we can be, which is always a plus when it comes to marriage and family.

Seek Help When You Come to An Impasse

An impasse is a situation in which no progress is possible, especially because of disagreement. There are times in almost every marriage when you reach a point when you need help. By far, the worst thing you can do is ignore a problem or issue. Sweeping things under a rug and hoping that they will go away, are ridiculous concepts. The only good way to handle a problem is to deal with it.

There are so many options available today for help. There are amazing Christian counselors, ministers, mentors, books, videos, workshops, seminars, and more. There are books that cover how to deal with just about every problem a marriage could face. Find one and read it; improve your marriage. Don't ignore an issue you may be facing.

There are all types of people reading this book ... people with good marriages, great marriages, and struggling marriages. If you find yourself in that last category, don't give up. Every marriage can improve, including yours. If it has taken some time to get your marriage in bad shape, then it may take some time to get your marriage back in good shape. Seek help when you need it.

You probably already know the answer to this question without us asking, but we will ask anyway. Between husbands and wives, which is least likely to want to get help when there is an issue? Ding-ding-ding! You guessed it right; the answer is - husbands.

A few years ago, I was riding in the car with a friend of mine who practices family medicine. For the sake of conversation, I asked, "Who is the most frustrating type of patient that you see?" He replied, "By far, it is men in their fifties." Being a man in my fifties, I cut my eyes around at him to see if he was being serious. He was.

I asked, "What is it about men in their fifties that is frustrating?" He replied, "Lots of them brag about never having been to a doctor. They have not had regular checkups, and they have not taken care of their body by eating right or exercising. When they begin to have problems, they come see me for the first time in years. After receiving lab results, I have to tell them they are borderline diabetic, have high blood pressure and high cholesterol. They are always a little surprised that they have so many problems and ask if there is a pill to fix it, so that they will be better tomorrow. I have to explain to them that it took a while to get themselves into this poor condition, and it will take them a while to get out of this condition. There is no quick fix. They will have to start taking some medicine, eating right, and exercising for the long haul."

The same thing holds true with marriage. If you haven't put out much effort over the last several years, you won't be able to fix things tomorrow. However, if you start making changes right now, you can improve things over time.

Think back to the introduction of this book when we talked about how marriage is like a rowboat. When both a husband and a wife are willing to pick up their paddles and row, a marriage can go amazing places. However, if no one is rowing, or if only one person is rowing, then that little boat just drifts down the river. Too many times we've seen marriages that have drifted until they reach a waterfall. The one that's been rowing and asking the other to help finally gives up and says, "Okay I'm done." Generally, that person has been asking for a long time to get help for the marriage through counseling or other means. All the while, the other person has been ignoring problems and sweeping them under a rug. When the waterfall comes, the person who has not been rowing picks up their paddle and frantically tries to save the boat before it goes over the waterfall. Often, they even complain that they are the only one trying to save the marriage, when their spouse has been begging for years that they seek help.

We urge you not to be that person who waits until the last second to pick up the paddle and row. Instead, reach for that paddle long before the boat gets to the waterfall. If your spouse asks about attending a workshop, seeking some counseling, or reading a book together, don't brush them off or get mad, be willing to do it.

Remember that your marriage is the most valuable thing you have. Make it your goal that one day you will hold your spouse's hand when you are eighty and say, "We made it."

Bonita

We have made several trips to the country of

Honduras over the past twelve years. On one of our trips, we had the privilege to feed a small community just outside the city dump. It was a very poor community, and we were handing out groceries to all the sweet families.

My friend, Troy Bradford, spotted an older Honduran man wearing a cap with an Amarillo, Texas insignia. Troy elbowed me, pointed out the man and said, "Hey look! How do you suppose a cap from Amarillo, Texas made it all the way to Honduras?" Troy decided he wanted a photograph and approached the man to ask permission. He nodded, and Troy took the picture of him wearing the Amarillo, Texas cap. After the photograph was taken, the Honduran man did what every person does when you take their picture; he wanted to see it in the viewfinder. Troy happily showed him his picture, and he nodded and smiled.

After looking at his picture, the man looked up and pointed out a woman who'd been through our grocery line. He asked Troy to take her picture as well. She was toothless, had gray hair, wrinkles, and wore an apron over her dirty red shirt. We had no clue why he wanted us to take her picture, but Troy asked permission, and she agreed. After taking the photograph, once again the Honduran man wanted to see the viewfinder. He wanted to see the picture of the woman.

When he saw it, he did something very unusual for a Honduran man. As he looked at the viewfinder, he became emotional. With teary eyes, he said one word over and over. "Bonita, oh bonita, bonita." The only word he could utter while looking at her picture was the word "bonita," which means pretty. We learned that she was his wife, and she was absolutely beautiful in his eyes. He didn't see a toothless old woman with a dirty shirt, wrinkles, and gray hair. He only saw one thing ... beauty.

Troy was emotional as he realized the old man was staring at a picture of his wife and seeing nothing but beauty in her. When we parted ways with the older couple, Troy said, "I want 'bonita' for my marriage." I replied, "Me too, Troy, me too!"

I want to look across the room at my wife when we are old and gray and see nothing but "bonita" ... no gray hair, no wrinkles, just the beautiful woman with whom I have shared an amazing life. I want to take her hand and say "We made it." We want that for your marriage as well!

We pray the things you have read in this book will bless you. Please know that in order for your marriage to be strengthened, you will have to be intentional at putting these basic Christian principles into practice. It will take more than merely reading suggestions in a marriage book.

You will have to take them to heart and do them. A great marriage doesn't happen by accident. It takes work, but it's so very worth it.

Now, pick up that boat paddle and row with all of your might!

ABOUT THE AUTHORS

Trey & Lea have been married over 30 years and have been involved in marriage and family ministry for most of that time. They have a strong presence on social media, and conduct their "Stronger Marriage" and "Stronger Families" workshops all over the United States. They talk to thousands of couples yearly about healthy marriages and families. Trey & Lea live in Childress, Texas, and have enjoyed raising four boys. You can learn more from their website: StrongerMarriageWorkshops.com. You can follow them on social media here:

twitter.com/StrongMarriage5
Instagram.com/Stronger_Marriages
Facebook.com/StrongerMarriageWorkshop

DISCUSSION QUESTIONS

Owning a membership to a gym but never using it doesn't do you any good. If you want to see results, you have to actually work out on a regular basis. If you want to build strength and remain strong, you have to consistently use each muscle group. That same principle holds true for your marriage. If you read the words in this book, but don't actually apply the tools we've given to strengthen your marriage, then your marriage will not grow stronger. Our hope is that you will use the ten marriage-strengthening principles in this book on a consistent basis, so that your marriage will grow stronger and stronger with each passing year. For each chapter, we have added discussion questions for individuals and couples. (These can also be used in a class or groups setting.)

CHAPTER 1 – KEEP PADDLING

STRENGTH TRAINING EXERCISES FOR YOUR MARRIAGE

1. We've titled this book, "10 Ways to a Stronger Marriage." Ten things can sound like a lot. You may be doing great at some of these ten things, while you may need to do some work on others. We can often be guilty of thinking, "My spouse really needs to work on this point," but we don't readily admit that we could use to improve on some things as well. Why do you suppose it's easier for us to notice what our spouse needs to improve, than it is to admit what we need to improve?

2. In chapter one, we explain a marriage stalemate ... when the husband and wife both refuse to make things better, or try to improve, if the other doesn't make the first move. Have you ever witnessed a marriage stalemate?

3. What are some reasons that couples don't paddle their side of the boat?

4. From chapter one, "Many married couples don't put any money, time, or effort into their marriage until problems surface. After problems arise, couples frantically start trying to invest time, money, and effort into their relationship with hopes to make it good again. Our point is this: don't wait until your marriage is having issues to start working on it. Work on your marriage during the good times, so there will be less bad times." Name some specific things you could do to improve and strengthen your marriage? (Hint: We'll help you with the first one ... you're doing one by reading this book. You can write that down. ☐)

5. "Don't give up. Don't stop paddling." Give a couple of reasons that you don't ever want to give up or stop working on your marriage.

CHAPTER 2 – KEEP UP THE CHASE

STRENGTH TRAINING EXERCISES FOR YOUR MARRIAGE

1. We discussed how you sent flowers, flirted, bragged on one another, dressed up for one another, dated, held hands, etc. before you were married. Why do you think many couples stop doing these things on a regular basis after they are married?

2. Wives, circle the things in the following list that you still enjoy, and men, underline the ones you still enjoy?

- Flirting
- Dating
- Holding hands
- Receiving flowers or other surprises
- Dressing up for one another before a date
- Spending time together
- Talking to one another
- Sending notes or texts

3. The love that God says is essential in marriage is an "action" love. The world's view of love believes things like "love is a feeling" and "we don't feel in love anymore." How does God's view and the world's view differ?

4. Name 3 things your spouse does that show love for you?

   Husbands:
   1.
   2.
   3.

   Wives:
   1.
   2.
   3.

5. DATING: Write about one or two of your favorite dates you've had with your spouse?

6. The following list is a great rule of thumb for dating. How close do you get on these? How could you improve?

    a. One date every two weeks.
    b. One overnight date every 6 months.
    c. One weekend away once a year.

7. Chapter 2 includes "12 Date Night Ideas." If you could pick 2 for this month, which two would be your choice?

8. Wives, on a scale of 1-10 (10 being the most), how important is non-sexual touch to you?

9. Husbands, on a scale of 1-10 (10 being the most), how important is it that your wife flirts with you?

CHAPTER 3 – TALKING IS NOT AN OPTION

STRENGTH TRAINING EXERCISES FOR YOUR MARRIAGE

"We were attracted to one another, but we didn't fall in love because of attraction. We fell in love through conversation, and when we continue to regularly talk and communicate, we keep that love alive. Catch this ... this is really important: Communication to a marriage is like oxygen to life. Without it, it dies."

1. Do you remember the long phone calls and conversations you had back when you were dating? List some of the things you talked about?

2. In your opinion, why is conversation so important to marriage?

3. How often do you sit down as a couple simply to talk to one another? Do you set time aside specifically for this purpose? Why or why not?

4. Husbands and wives often have different communication styles. Have you found this true in your marriage? How do you work through the challenges this can bring? Who is the bigger talker?

5. In the chapter, I mentioned failing at trying to multitask while listening to Lea. When it comes to listening to your spouse, what are some of the distractions you often face?

6. Write out James 1:19. Why is this verse, especially the part about listening, important in marriage?

CHAPTER 4 – HEAP IT ON THICK

STRENGTH TRAINING EXERCISES FOR YOUR MARRIAGE

Newlyweds do a great job overlooking the flaws of their spouse, while focusing on their positive traits. People who have been married for a while tend to do the opposite ... noticing all of their spouse's flaws, while overlooking their positive traits.

1. Would your spouse define you as a glass half-full or a glass half-empty person?

2. Why do you suppose that we find it easier to see our spouse's flaws and weaknesses?

3. Wives, before we mentioned it in the chapter, had you already noticed that your husband loves your praise for even the smallest stuff?

4. In the chapter, we mention a study that shows couples, who give five times more praise than

criticism, are much less likely to divorce. Name three things that you appreciate about your spouse...

    a. HUSBANDS:

-
-
-

    b. WIVES:

-
-
-

5. Wives, when it comes to praise, how can you improve at heaping it on thick?

CHAPTER 5 – LET'S GET NAKED, BUT NOT THAT WAY!

STRENGTH TRAINING EXERCISES FOR YOUR MARRIAGE

1. If you had to define "marriage," what words would you use? What makes marriage unique and different from any other human relationship?

2. Write out Genesis 2:25.

3. In your opinion, why is nakedness/openness so important in marriage?

4. People often ask us what our rules are for phones. Here's what we say: As for us, both of our phones are open to the other at any time. We can pick up one another's phone and feel free to use it. We have nothing to hide from one another. That being said, we never feel the need to go through the other's phone, BUT IF our spouse wanted to do so, that would be totally fine. Do you agree or disagree with this? Why?

5. Would you agree that emotional affairs through texting/messaging are a problem today? What can a couple do the guard against this?

6. Can you think of a reason one spouse should ever lock the other spouse out of their phone?

7. If someone was to look at any of your social media accounts, what are some of the things they would see you passionate about? What do you post about most often? How often do you post pictures of you and your spouse?

8. It seems that 9 affairs out of 10 start with "We're just friends." What are ways in which married couples can have healthy boundaries with friends of the opposite sex?

CHAPTER 6 – LET'S GET NAKED, YES THAT WAY!

STRENGTH TRAINING EXERCICES FOR YOUR MARRIAGE

1. Why do you feel that the world is comfortable talking about sex, but Christians are not?

2. You've probably thought of sex as being for pleasure and procreation, but have you thought of sex as being for protection from temptation? Having sex on a regular basis, doesn't mean you won't be tempted, but according to Paul in 1 Corinthians 7, it can help. Is this a new concept for you?

3. Speaking of frequency, the regulator of sex in your marriage shouldn't be the one with the lower sex drive. Frequency should be a mutual decision between the husband and wife. Strive to meet in the middle. Are you both comfortable with the frequency of sex in your marriage?

4. In about 80% of marriages, men have the higher sex drive than women. In this chapter, we discussed how "men are often like microwaves," and "women are often like slow-cookers." Does that analogy fit your marriage? Wives, what are some "little things" your husband does throughout the day that turn you on?

5. Dr. Kevin Leman believes that sex's biggest enemy for women is busyness and weariness. Do you agree? What are some things you can specifically do to overcome this issue?

6. Scheduling sex has worked for us when we were struggling to find time. Some think scheduling sex will take the spontaneity out of it, but can't you agree that scheduling sex, and having it, is better than not scheduling it and never getting around to it?

7. Read the book of Song of Songs in your Bible together this week. It probably won't take you more than 30 minutes. While reading, take note of all the sexual innuendos.

CHAPTER 7 – TREAT YOUR SPOUSE BETTER THAN THEY DESERVE

STRENGTH TRAINING EXERCISES FOR YOUR MARRIAGE

1. We listed many of our differences at the beginning of the chapter. What are some of your differences?

2. What are some ways that your differences can actually benefit your marriage?

3. Trey's love language is physical touch, while Lea's is acts of service. Do you both know each other's love language? What are they? If you don't know, Google "5 Love Language Test" and take the test for couples. It doesn't take long.

4. In your own words, why is speaking your spouse's love language so important?

5. Take a moment to write one another a note. Tell what it is you love and appreciate about the other.

CHAPTER 8 – FIRST THINGS FIRST

STRENGTH TRAINING EXERCISES FOR YOUR MARRIAGE

1. No one ever deliberately puts their marriage on the back burner, yet we do it. We allow lots of less important things to take priority. Why do you feel we allow this to happen?

2. We visit with people all the time who didn't realize their marriage was the most valuable thing they had until it was threatened or lost. When you make a list of your earthly assets, you may never think to include your marriage and family, but there is really nothing more important. How can it make a difference to see them as an asset all the time, instead of just when there is a threat of losing them?

3. Do your children see you only in your role as parents, or do they also see you as husband and wife? What percentage would you say is mom/dad, and what percentage is husband/wife?

4. Why is it important for your children to see you modeling marriage in a positive way?

5. When it comes to teaching your children about marriage, what are some areas that you need to improve in order to set a better example?

6. There are no perfect marriages because there are no perfect people. With that in mind, forgiveness has to play an essential part in every marriage. We understand that some marriages are crushed by affairs, addictions, and repeated offences. Sometimes it seems impossible to move on and forgive. Forgiveness isn't just for your spouse; it is for you as well. Holding a grudge against your spouse for past mistakes not only hurts you but also your marriage. Continually bringing up past hurts will poison the present and future with your spouse. Name something (or some things) you may still be holding against your spouse that you need to forgive. Now pray about it. Also, name something (or things) that you may feel your spouse still holds against you. What can you do to help them with this?

7. We closed this chapter by talking about our wedding rings. Do you wear yours? Why or why not? What does your wedding ring mean to you?

CHAPTER 9 – FRIENDSHIP MATTERS

STRENGTH TRAINING EXERCISES FOR YOUR MARRIAGE

1. One of the biggest myths in marriage is "absence makes the heart grow fonder." The reason this is a myth is that long absences are actually very hard on your marriage. It's hard to have a close friendship with someone you don't spend much time with. The same is true in your marriage. Friendship is one of the glues of a healthy marriage, but it's hard to be friends if you never spend any time together. List 3 or 4 things you love to do with your spouse. (Bonus if you can come up with 10)

2. What's something new you love to do with your spouse?

3. We mentioned in this chapter, "If it's important to your spouse, it should be important to you." This is true whether it's your spouse's hobbies or their need for emotional support such as communication, sex, affection, etc. In your own words, why is this important?

4. Why are regular date nights important to remaining best friends?

5. Spending time together is important to building a friendship, but so is communication. Why is it important to your friendship that you talk and share about things in your everyday life?

6. Is there anything keeping you from spending more time together? Money? Babysitters? Schedules? What suggestions did we give in the chapter that you can try? The Bible talks about the value of friendship in your marriage: "*Two are better than one, because they have a good return for their labor: If either of them falls down, one can help the other up. But pity anyone who falls and has no one to help them up. Also, if two lie down together, they will keep warm. But how can one keep warm alone? Though one may be overpowered, two can defend themselves.*" (Ecclesiastes 4:9-12a, NIV). One of the reasons that God created marriage was so we could have a lifelong friend. Rewrite this verse in your own words to specifically reflect friendship in marriage.

CHAPTER 10 – THE OVERLOOKED INTIMACY

STRENGTH TRAINING EXERCISES FOR YOUR MARRIAGE

1. For many men, when you mention intimacy, they immediately think of sex. In this chapter, we discussed spiritual intimacy - one of the most overlooked and most important forms of intimacy available to married couples. Have you ever given much thought to the importance of spiritual intimacy?

2. On a scale of 1-10, where would you rank how well you are doing on spiritual intimacy in your marriage?

3. What are your spiritual intimacy strengths? In what areas of spiritual intimacy do you need improvement as a couple?

4. Storms will come ... Jesus said so in Matthew 7:24-27. What's the key to your house/home/family surviving the storms?

5. What are reasons that some married couples struggle to pray with one another? Is this an issue in your marriage?

6. All seven of the things listed in the chapter to pray for your family are essential! Take a minute and put them in order of importance to you.

7. When it comes to seeking help with issues in marriage, why do you suppose husbands, more so than wives, are hesitant to ask for help?

8. Will you take our challenge to briefly pray together at bedtime every night? Take turns each night. Remember it's okay to keep it simple and short.

NOTES

CHAPTER 2

1. Karen Lehnardt, "63 Blissful Marriage Facts," www.factretreiver.com/marriage-facts (November 22, 2016; updated September 7, 2019)

CHAPTER 3

1. Steven R. Covey, *The 7 Habits of Highly Effective People: Powerful Lessons in Personal Change,* (New York: Free Press, 15th edition, 2004)

CHAPTER 4

1. Kyle Benson, "The Magic Ratio, According to Science," The Gottman Institute, www.gottman.com/blog/the-magic-relatioship-ratio-according-science/ (October 4, 2017)
2. Richard and JeannaLynn May, What God Has Joined Ministries, www.amayzingimpact.com/

CHAPTER 5

1. Interesting Literature, "The Curious Origin of the Word 'Unfriend'," https://interestingliterature.com/2016/04/22/the-curious-origin-of-the-word-unfriend/

CHAPTER 6

1. Strange But True, "How Big Is the Porn Industry?," https://medium.com/@Strange_bt_True/how-big-is-the-porn-industry-fbc1ac78091b (February 19, 2017)

2. Shaunti Feldhahn, "When She Has the Stronger Sex Drive; Part 1," https://shaunti.com/2015/11/when-she-has-the-stronger-sex-drive-part-one/ (November 12, 2015)
3. Dr. Kevin Leman, *Sheet Music: Uncovering the Secrets to Sexual Intimacy in Marriage (Carol Stream, Illinois:* Tyndale House publishers, Inc., 2003, 2008), 183
4. Ibid., 188-189

CHAPTER 7

1. Dr. Gary Chapman, *The 5 Love Languages: The Secret to Love That Lasts*, (Chicago: Northfield, 2009)
2. https://www.5lovelanguages.com/profile/couples/
3. Pam Farrell, Jean E. Jones, Karla Dornacher, Discovering Joy in Philippians (Eugene, Oregon: Harvest House Publishers, 2019)

CHAPTER 9

1. Shawn Grover and John F. Helliwell, "How's Life at Home? New Evidence on Marriage and the Set Point for Happiness," www.nber.org/papers/w20794 (December 2014)
2. Dr. Willard Harley, Recreation Enjoyment Inventory, marriagebuildres.com/recreation-enjoyment-inventory.html